ABOR

ABORIGINAL
MYTHS

Tales of the Dreamtime

A. W. REED

REED

REED
Part of William Heinemann Australia
Level 9, North Tower
1–5 Railway Street
Chatswood NSW 2067

First published 1978
Reprinted 1982, 1984, 1987, 1988, 1989, 1991, 1992

© A.W. Reed 1978

National Library of Australia
Cataloguing-in-Publication Data

Aboriginal myths.
 ISBN 0 7301 0201 7
 (1) Aborigines, Australian – Legends. 1. Reed,
 Alexander Wyclif, 1908-   comp.
398.20994

Printed in Australia by Griffin Paperbacks, Adelaide

CONTENTS

INTRODUCTION

ACCORDING to the *Concise Oxford Dictionary*, a myth is a 'purely fictitious narrative usually involving supernatural persons etc, and embodying popular ideas on natural phenomena'.

In this collection emphasis has been placed on myths that attempt to explain the origins of natural phenomena while a companion volume, *Aboriginal Legends*,* deals with legends as distinct from myths. The distinction is tenuous. Resorting to the dictionary again, we find that a legend is a 'traditional story popularly regarded as historical, myth, such literature or tradition . . .'

While the definition is adequate for most purposes, it fails to differentiate between myth and legend. The terms are not precisely synonymous. In dealing with Aboriginal subjects in the series in which this book is included, legends, as distinct from myths, may be regarded as folklore, i.e. in the nature of fireside tales, that include some miraculous or supernatural element. Myths usually deal with whatever pantheon of gods may be believed in and, frequently, attempt to explain the 'origins' of a variety of phenomena.

The first part of the present book deals with acts of creation as exemplified in the deeds of the Great Spirit or All-Father; the second with those of totemic ancestors; the third (which approaches more closely to legends) with tales of the origin of certain natural phenomena and specific features of animal life. In most cases names of animals have been capitalised to indicate totemic ancestors. Few of the tales are confined to a single category, and distinction between the three topics is blurred, the division being one of convenience.

An attempt has been made to convey some idea of the mystical bond that existed between man, his environment, and the spirit life of the Dreamtime. Even the homelier tales in the last section are imbued with that 'oneness' that links all living creatures in a spiritual relationship.

_____
* A. W. Reed (A. H. & A. W. Reed).

A certain 'westernisation' of the traditional tales must be admitted. In some cases they are the retelling of twice-told tales; in others the story may be adapted and enlarged from the transcript of a myth or legend recorded directly from an Aboriginal teller of tales. In such circumstances, particularly in more recent times, the original myth may already have suffered a number of changes. Again, it should be remembered that a favourite tradition may have been preserved in song and dance rather than or in addition to the spoken form.

A fragment of legend from the Katherine River district illustrates the difficulty of adaptation to another culture:

> He-came came into-cave budidjonanaiwan (a kind of wallaby) that-one? went Ganwulu. From-Ganwulu (to) Nganyordabmag from-there (to) Nganyoron. From-Nganyoron (to) Nganwaragbregbregmi. He-went-down into-cave at-Ninganda. To-the-cave (of) Ninganda not he-went-in. Children (and) women not-allowed, white-man (?ghost) cannot? shut-up, make play, (?blow). Not come-out cannot-go-out cannot-depart-altogether.*

This fragment has been paraphrased by Dr A. Capell who points out that Nganwaragbregbregmi was stated to mean 'where the dingo broke his shoulder and cried out', but that the story of the giving of the name was not collected. 'The sand-wallaby came and went into the cave. He went to Ganwulu, and from there to Nganyordabmag and thence to Nganyoron. From Nganyoron he went to Nganwaragbregbregmi. At Ninganda he went down to a cave. He did not go into the Ninganda cave. Children and women are not allowed to go to that cave.'

Fortunately there is infinite variety in the Dreamtime tales. The Aranda traditions collected by Professor T. G. H. Strehlow preserve their beauty and poetry in translation. Similarly, there is singular charm in some of the renderings of stories by modern Aboriginals retold by Roland Robinson. Every writer who ventures to retell Aboriginal myths and legends must adopt his own style and presentation. For my part, I have rewritten a

---

* A. W. Reed, *An Illustrated Encyclopedia of Aboriginal Life* (A. H. & A. W. Reed), quoting *Oceania*, vol 30, no 3, p. 218.

variety of myths and folk tales with sincere admiration for the men of old who gave pleasure and inspiration to their fellow tribesmen. Profiting by the research of others I have retold them simply, as they appeal to me, and with only sufficient change to make them acceptable to present day readers. If by chance they give enjoyment to others and a little insight into the treasury of Aboriginal lore, something will have been gained.

I am deeply indebted to the writings of T. G. H. Strehlow, R. M. and C. H. Berndt, Ursula McConnel, Roland Robinson, Aldo Massola, W. E. Harney, Mildred Norledge and others, together with those of missionaries, field-workers, and enthusiasts of earlier generations, for recording many tales of the Dreamtime and helping to preserve part of the diverse cultures of the Aboriginal people of Australia.

It should also be mentioned that two or three stories that appear in *Myths and Legends of Australia** have been retold in this collection.

A. W. REED

_____

* A. W. Reed (A. H. & A. W. Reed).

PART ONE

THE GREAT FATHER

SEPARATED by some two thousand kilometres of ocean, and with different racial characteristics, some interesting comparisons can be made between the Aboriginals of Australia and the Maoris of New Zealand. In New Zealand the famous field-worker Elsdon Best once stated that the Maori people (one of the several branches of the Polynesians) had taken the first step towards monotheism in their belief that Io was the Divine Father of Mankind, the uncreated, the creator, omnipotent and omniscient. The Io cult was an esoteric belief known only to the highest grade of Tohunga (priest), and possibly only to those of certain tribes. Those who had not been trained in the whare wananga, the school of sacred lore, were unaware even of the name of the highest and holiest of gods, being content with a pantheon of departmental gods who controlled the forces of nature, and groups of lesser deities.

In order to form even an approximate comparison between Maoris and Australian Aboriginals, it is necessary to consider the environment of the two ethnic groups. Nature was kind to the Maoris. It provided them with an equable climate in a land where birds and fish were in abundant supply. Bracken root, unpalatable though it might be, was a staple form of diet, available at all seasons; while in northern districts the kumara or sweet potato, brought from tropical islands of the Pacific, could be cultivated in specially prepared plantations. The availability of food from forest, lake, river, and sea therefore encouraged settlement. With permanent buildings in which to sleep, meet, and hold special 'schools' for candidates for the priesthood, and with a common language, it was not surprising that over the centuries they developed a distinctive culture, which is today summed up in the word maoritanga.

In striking contrast, the forebears of the Aboriginals had come to a land that varied immensely in its physical features and climate, from the harsh environment of the Centre, to

11

dense steamy jungle, and the more temperate regions of the south-east. Over a large area, life was an unending struggle against a seemingly hostile environment. The outstanding feature of this so-called primitive race of people is their adaptation to these conditions.

The environment that white Australians regard as barren and hostile and incapable of sustaining human life, was home to the Aboriginal, at least that part of it that belonged to his totemic ancestor. Away from that familiar territory he was indeed virtually lost and defenceless. Within it he was part of it, attuned to its every mood, relaxed, under the most gruelling experiences, confident in his oneness with the spirit and presence of the ancestor, living a full life in the region created for him and all who preceded and succeeded him.

The concept of a Father Spirit, which was held by some of the larger tribes, a deity who was before and beyond even the ancestors, was therefore an astounding leap of the human mind and spirit from the material to the divine.

It may be objected that this is a romanticised view of the Aboriginal mind, far removed from the harsh conditions, and cruel practices such as those of the initiation ceremonies. It is inescapable that man is to some extent the product of his environment, and that when his survival is at stake, finer feelings and humane practices must be subordinated to the need to exist and to continue the life of the clan, moiety, social group, or tribe to which he belongs. It is equally true that the realities of life in his particular environment will enter into the stories he composes and the beliefs he inherits.

Although worship in its more refined forms was unknown to the Aboriginal, he shared his existence with the supernatural powers to which he owed his life—and is this not a form of worship that might set an example to many in our present civilisation who have abandoned religion for materialism?

The 'environmental impact', varying from one part of the continent to another, resulted in separation and a considerable degree of isolation of the various tribes, leading in turn to the evolution of distinct dialects and languages, thereby inhibiting communication and intensifying the isolation of individual communities. As each tribe had its own ancestor who journeyed through a particular territory, forming its physical features in the Dreamtime and entrusting them to his descendants, so each had his own name and characteristics, and so, also, had the Great Father Spirit who is a sovereign god known by different names. The concept is not universal, but was widely spread in the south-east of the continent.

Aldo Massola in *Bunjil's Cave** has listed several of the Great Spirits known to the tribes. He points out that each sent a son to earth to carry out his designs for mankind and care for them, and to punish evil-doers. To the criticism that this concept has arisen as a result of missionary teaching, he points out that the sacred knowledge relating to the Father Spirit has come from the 'old men' and that it is unlikely that this theory is soundly based. The names of the Great Spirits he refers to are:

Baiame (there are several variations in spelling—Baiame, Byamee, and others), known to the Ya-itma-thang of the High Plains (and widely through the south-eastern regions); and his son Daramulun (or Gayandi).

Nooralie of the Murray River region and his son Gnawdenoorte.

Mungan Ngour of the Kurnai of Queensland and his son Tundun.

Bunjil (there are several spellings of the name) of the Kulin and of the Wotjobaluk and his son Bimbeal, or Gargomitch.

Pern-mehial of the Mara of the Western Desert and his son Wirtin-wirtin-jaawan.

To these could be added others such as Karora and his many sons, Nurunderi, Goin, and Biral. Of the many individual tribal myths of the Great Father, three have been selected—those of Baiame, Punjel or Bunjil, and Nurunderi.

Baiame

ONE of the many significant features of Baiame is that he is the incarnation of kindness and care for others, and that he has the distinction of having elevated Birrahgnooloo, one of his wives, to a position which may be described as Mother-of-All, to live

---

* Lansdowne Press.

with him in the sky for all time. As Mrs Langloh Parker has said, 'She, like him, had a totem for each part of her body; no one totem can claim her, but all do.'

Having made a world in which man and the animal could live, Baiame looked at it and, in the majestic words of the first chapter of Genesis, 'he saw everything he had made, and, behold, it was very good'.

Baiame and the First Man and Woman

AND again like the Lord God, Baiame walked on the earth he had made, among the plants and animals, and created man and woman to rule over them. He fashioned them from the dust of the ridges, and said,

'These are the plants you shall eat—these and these, but not the animals I have created.'

Having set them in a good place, the All-Father departed.

To the first man and woman, children were born and to them in turn children who enjoyed the work of the hands of Baiame. His world had begun to be populated, and men and women praised Baiame for providing for all their needs. Sun and rain brought life to the plants that provided their sustenance.

All was well in the world they had received from the bountiful provider, until a year when the rain ceased to fall. There was little water. The flowers failed to fruit, leaves fell from the dry, withered stems, and there was hunger in the land—a new and terrifying experience for men, women, and little children who had never lacked for food and drink.

In desperation a man killed some of the forbidden animals, and shared the kangaroo-rats he had caught with his wife. They offered some of the flesh to one of their friends but, remembering Baiame's prohibition, he refused it. The man was ill with hunger. They did their best to persuade him to eat, but he remained steadfast in his refusal. At length, wearying of their importunity, he staggered to his feet, turning his back on the tempting food, and walked away.

Shrugging their shoulders, the husband and wife went on with their meal. Once they were satisfied, they thought again of their friend and wondered whether they could persuade him to eat. Taking the remains of the meal with them, they followed his trail. It led across a broad plain and disappeared at the edge of a river. They wondered how he had crossed it and, more importantly, how they themselves could cross. In spite of the fact that it had dwindled in size, owing to the prolonged drought, it was running too swiftly for them to wade or swim.

They could see him, some little distance away on the farther side, lying at the foot of a tall gum tree. They were on the point of turning back when they saw a coal-black figure, half man half beast, dropping from the branches of the tree and stooping over the man who was lying there. They shouted a warning, but were too far away for him to hear, even if he were awake. The black monster picked up the inert body, carried it up into the branches and disappeared. They could only think that the tree trunk was hollow and that the monster had retreated to its home with his lifeless burden.

One event succeeded another with bewildering rapidity. A puff of smoke billowed from the tree. The two frightened observers heard a rending sound as the tree lifted itself from the ground, its roots snapping one by one, and soared across the river, rising as it took a course to the south. As it passed by they had a momentary glimpse of two large, glaring eyes within its shadow, and two white cockatoos with frantically flapping wings, trying to catch up with the flying tree, straining to reach the shelter of its branches.

Within minutes the tree, the cockatoos, and the glaring eyes had dwindled to a speck, far to the south, far above their heads.

For the first time since creation, death had come to one of the men whom Baiame had created, for the monster within the tree trunk was Yowee, the Spirit of Death.

In the desolation of a drought-stricken world, all living things mourned because a man who was alive was now as dead as the kangaroo-rats that had been killed for food. Baiame's intention for the men and animals he loved had been thwarted. 'The swamp oak trees sighed incessantly, the gum trees shed tears of blood, which crystallised as red gum,' wrote Roland Robinson, in relating this legend of the Kamilroi tribe in his book *Wandjina*.* 'To this day,' he continued, 'to the tribes of

---

* Lansdowne Press.

15

that part is the Southern Cross known as "Yaraandoo"—the place of the White Gum tree—and the Pointers as "Mouyi", the white cockatoos.'

It was a sad conclusion to the hopes of a world in the making, but the bright cross of the Southern Cross is a sign to men that there is a place for them in the limitless regions of space, the home of the All-Father himself, and that beyond death lies a new creation.

Baiame and the Bullroarer

ONE of Baiame's many accomplishments was the fashioning of the first bullroarer. To those who know it only as a child's toy, the statement will no doubt be surprising; but to those who realise something of its significance in sacred ceremonies and the care taken to hide it from prying eyes, the legend that ascribes its invention to the All-Father will add to the respect that must be shown to it. It is the voice of Baiame. No woman was allowed to see it and in speaking of it, women were not permitted to use the same word as men. In one district men called it gayandi (a name that has great significance), the women gurraymi. Both words are said to mean 'bora spirit'. Bora is a term used originally in New South Wales, but now applied generally throughout eastern Australia to the secret ground or ring in which initiation ceremonies (again forbidden to women) were performed. Professor Elkin believed that the smaller bora represented the sky world, and was therefore linked with the dwelling place of Baiame.

One of the functions of smaller bullroarers was to attract women, as portrayed so vividly in Dame Mary Gilmore's poem 'The Song of the Woman-Drawer':

> I am the woman-drawer;
> Pass me not by;
> I am the secret voice:
> Hear ye me cry;
> I am that power which might
> Looses abroad;
> I am the root of life;
> I am the chord.

More important than their ability as 'woman-drawers' was the fact that the sound of these sacred artifacts was the utterance of Baiame. Speaking in the voice of the Dreamtime, they warned the uninitiated from the bora ground. Because they symbolised the one who had created them and, in the initiation, was drawing them to himself, they were the means by which initiated men were linked together in a spiritual unity. Young men undergoing the painful ordeal of initiation heard the wailing of the bullroarers in the distance as they left the camp where women had been confined. The bullroarers spoke in unuttered words that only the wisest men could interpret, telling of acceptance or rejection in the ritual of death and rebirth in the sacred life of grown men.

In manufacturing the prototype, the skill of Baiame was put to the test. He wished to provide an instrument that was his own, yet one that men could use. It was to be his voice, yet it must have material form, with sufficient substance to knock out the front teeth of young men who were preparing to be accepted into the ranks of men.

Baiame's first attempt was not successful. In adapting his creation to the needs of man, he was too ambitious. He made a stone image in the form of a man, and placed it in the first bora. The figure, which represented his son, was therefore called Gayandi or, among some tribes, Darramulun. As the representation of a son of the Sky-Father it was endued with life, while still retaining the composition of stone.

Gayandi was soon found to be far too strong and vigorous to preside over the bora ground. He was successful in knocking out front teeth, but when he began to eat the faces of the initiates, Baiame realised that his enthusiasm must be restrained. He therefore changed the stone figure into a living animal, somewhat like an echidna, with hair on its back instead of spines. In doing so, he went to the opposite extreme, for this peculiar animal refused to remain in the bora circle. It trotted into the bush and has never since been seen. Nevertheless its spirit remains, a devil that lives to injure mankind. It lurks near bora grounds, always remaining in hiding. If it touches a man or boy (or even a shadow), that person will be affected with a rash from which no one has ever recovered.

Baiame's next attempt was to fashion a stone bullroarer to

simulate his voice. It was smaller than the image of Gayandi, but was sufficient to crack a man's skull if he approached too close. Unfortunately it proved too heavy for men to wield.*

After these unsuccessful experiments Baiame abandoned his quest, perhaps waiting for further inspiration. The answer came unexpectedly, just as men often find their problems solved in unexpected ways.

Baiame was chopping firewood in the Sky-land, for even there the nights can be cold. When men see the myriads of sparks of the sky-fires they are aware that the spirits of the sky have lit many fires to warm themselves. Baiame was felling a coolabah tree with such energy that chips flew in every direction. Occasionally one would spin through the air, emitting a humming sound that varied only with the speed or the size of the splinter.

'Oh! Here is the answer to my problem,' Baiame thought. He gathered a handful of the chips that had produced this peculiar sound and examined them closely, sorting them into several shapes, some long, straight, and narrow, others broader and oval. Selecting a straight piece he trimmed it to shape and smoothed it back and front, pierced a hole at one end, and threaded it on a stout cord. Another he fashioned to a different profile and from another kind of wood. When they were finished he hung them from the branches of the coolabah tree and went to his camp to see whether his evening meal was ready.

During the night the wind rose. His wives sat up, staring into the darkness and huddling together. They had heard a new voice in the sky and were afraid. They woke Baiame.

'Help us!' they said. 'A strange spirit has come to the coolabah tree you cut down today. What shall we do?'

'Listen to it,' Baiame said. 'What does it sound like?'

'Like a voice speaking, but we can't hear the words.'

'Whose voice do you think it sounds like?' Baiame asked.

They looked at each other and said nothing until the youngest wife, who was bolder than the others, said reluctantly,

'I cannot tell. It sounded like your voice—but that is ridiculous.'

---

* Small stone bullroarers have been seen but were rare. Wooden ones ranged in length from 12 centimetres to a metre in length and 2 to 10 centimetres in width. They seldom exceeded 6 millimetres in thickness.

'Not as ridiculous as you think,' Baiame said, and laughed until the booming sound echoed from the farthest bounds of the sky.

'Now run away and hide. What you have heard is indeed my voice. That is all you need to know.'

The women hurried away, while Baiame went to the coolabah tree where he had hung the two bullroarers. They were vibrating, spinning round the axis of the cord by which they were attached to the tree, and emitting the strange noise that had been heard for the first time in the realm of heaven.

'You are my Gayandi, and Gayandi is my voice,' he said as he untied them and carried them down to earth, where he gave them to the first men of the first bora ring. He warned them to treat them with reverence, to hide them when not in use, and showed them how to swing them in circles when they wished to receive a message from him.

'These are my Gayandi,' he said solemnly. 'You must protect them with your lives. No stranger, no woman, may ever see them. I will teach your wirinun, your clever-men, how to bring them alive to speak to you. They are the finest gifts I have ever made. You must treasure them.'

And so, for thousands of years, Baiame has spoken to his people, not with his own voice, but through the voice of the sacred bullroarer.

Baiame and Man

LIGHT was brought into the dark world by Yhi, the goddess of the sun. As few living things can grow without light, there was a close association between the two great spirits, Yhi and Baiame. Light and warmth were necessary for the preservation and growth of the animate world of Baiame's creation, and these were provided by Yhi. Yet light and warmth alone were insufficient for the making of mankind. Another dimension was needed, something more than the instinct that directed the actions of animals. That indefinable element could be supplied only by the All-Father who, in the beginning of the Dreamtime, could be described as thought, intelligence, even life itself.

Baiame had no corporeal body, nor did he need one until the time came to show himself to the beings he had formed. He was part of his creation, part of every single animal, and yet he was Baiame, indivisible and complete.

He confided his intentions to Yhi.

'I must clothe myself in flesh that is recognisably that of both man and god,' he said. 'My whole mind must be put into something that has life and is worthy of the gift. It must be a new creation.'

From the processes of thought, the joining together of atoms and microscopic grains of dust, the forming of blood and sinews, cartilege and flesh, and the convolutions of the substance of the brain, he formed an animal that walked erect on two legs. It had hands that could fashion tools and weapons and the wit to use them; above all, it had a brain that could obey the impulses of the spirit; and so Man, greatest of the animals, was fashioned as a vessel for the mind-power of the Great Spirit.

No other eye saw the making of Man, and the minutes of eternity went by in the last and greatest act of creation. The world became dark and sorrowful. Floods ravaged the land, animals took refuge in a cave high up in the mountains. From time to time one of them went to the entrance to see if the floods had subsided. There was nothing to be seen except the emptiness of the land and the endless swirling of the waters under a sunless sky.*

Yhi had turned her face from the birthpangs of spirit in man. As sunlight faded from the earth and the cave of refuge became black as night, the animals were bewildered. One after the other they went to the mouth of the cave, peering through the gloom, straining their eyes looking for something—a light—or a shape—that would explain the change that had come to the world.

Goanna was the first to report something that brought even more confusion to their rudimentary minds.

'A round, shining light,' he said. 'Like the moon. Perhaps it is the moon and the darkness is only an untimely night.'

---

* A. W. Reed, *Myths and Legends of Australia* (A. H. & A. W. Reed).

'Where is this light?' asked Eagle-hawk.

'Here, outside the cave, floating in the air, but close to the ground.'

'The moon is far up in the sky where the Great Father lives,' Eagle-hawk objected.

'I said "Like the moon",' Goanna retorted. 'It is like a light. Come and see for yourself.'

The animals were surprised when he came back and said, 'It's nothing like a light. You must be dreaming, Goanna.'

'What is it like?' came a voice from the back of the cave.

'It's a kangaroo.'

The laughter of the animals boomed in the confines of the cave.

'What's unusual about a kangaroo?'

'There's something very unusual about this kangaroo,' Eagle-hawk said, taking no notice of the laughter. 'Its eyes are as bright as stars. Their light pierced right through me.'

There was a rush to the mouth of the cave. They returned, arguing, quarrelling, shouting, contradicting each other. A strange presence had made a different impression on each undeveloped mind.

Baiame was disappointed. These were his creatures, yet none of them could recognise him. To each he appeared in a different guise. They were still quarrelling among themselves. The little portion of Baiame that was in each of his creation had failed to recognise him in all his fullness.

The quarrel had been even more serious than he had realised. Words had led to acts of violence. Claw and tooth had rent and torn. Dead animals lay on the floor of the cave.

Saddened by the consequences of his revelation, Baiame left them. The animals came out of the cave and, in a last supreme effort, he revealed himself in the form of a man. And in man, animals recognised the wisdom and majesty of the spirit of Baiame. Yhi flooded the world again with light.

The spirit of the All-Father returned to his home in the sky, leaving behind him the crown of his creation, man, who walked on two legs instead of four, who carried his head high, and inherited Baiame's capacity for thought and action.

Man was the master. He possessed tools and weapons that

other animals lacked—yet he was dissatisfied. Something was missing in his life. He observed the animals mating and knew that this was the missing element. The affinity he shared with Baiame, and which was present in birds, animals and even insects, had no human outlet. In this one respect he felt he was less than the animals.

One night he had a vivid dream. He had lain down at the foot of a yacca tree. As he looked at it in the last moments of consciousness, it must have impressed itself on his mind, for in his dream the tree was still there. The elongated flower spike rose far above his head, looking somewhat like a kangaroo's tail. From the old leaves at the base of the trunk came an aromatic perfume so strong that he was almost intoxicated.

The tree was moving, changing shape. He felt that if he took his eyes off it for a moment it would vanish. The flower spike was growing smaller, the trunk divided into two separate limbs, two more branches sprouted from beneath the flower. The bark grew soft and smooth as the flower separated into head and trunk. The transformation was complete. Another man had been created from a flowering tree and was stepping out of the grassy clump with arms outstretched to greet him.

But was it a man? This figure, more graceful than the grass-tree from which it came, was like man and yet unlike. More gently formed and rounded. With a flash of insight imparted by Baiame, man realised that this creature was woman, equal to man, and complementary both in nature and in form. The same divine spark illuminated her face and her thought as in man himself. He knew instinctively that in her was the otherness that separated and yet linked male and female in all life, and that they were both linked to the everlasting otherness that was part of Baiame himself.

They came together and embraced. Their feet scarcely touched the ground in the primal dance with which they celebrated their union. It was no longer a dream but reality. The dance was ended. With heaving breasts and arms round each other's bodies, they stood still to survey the world they now knew had been created for them, and which they shared with the All-Father.

'Not yours alone,' a distant voice proclaimed. 'Yours and mine. We are linked together for all time, you and your children and the reborn babies of the spirit world, and those I shall send after me. Look around you.'

They looked, and to their surprise saw that the plain was covered with plants and animals, standing motionless, listening to the words that proclaimed the ordering of Baiame's universe.

The voice continued. 'These are all my creatures, great and small, plant and animal, on land and in sea and sky. My creatures, made for your use and for you to care for. They will supply all your needs. They share in small measure the life that is in me, and now in full measure in you who are man and woman. This day is a beginning, for you and for me.'

The voice died away. There seemed to be a new kindliness in the sunlight of Yhi. From the plain about them came a vast and soft sighing. The spell that had held the animals motionless was broken. They scampered away and were lost to sight. Only the trees and grass and flowers remained in their places, equally aware of the coming of mankind.

The loneliness, the incompleteness was ended. The duties and obligations of man had begun. As the days and years went by, their shared existence took shape. He was the hunter, the maker of shelter. She was food-gatherer, home-maker, bearer of children. They worked, and danced, and played, and loved together and in them Baiame found fulfilment.

'In them I am content at last to show myself to the universe I have created,' he mused.

Baiame and Marmoo

IN the earliest Dreamtime, all was not well in the world that Baiame had made. Hills and valleys, stark mountain ranges, crystal-clear streams and rivers, and bare plains that slipped over distant horizons paid tribute to the patient hands of the master architect. Flowers of a thousand colours and shapes had been planted ready for the coming of man, while butterflies fluttered over the shaggy carpet of trees and reeds and grass. Wind played with clouds, sending vagrant patterns of light and shade across the land, where animals romped and sought their food. By day the goddess Yhi smiled as plants lifted their heads and young grasses reached towards her from the dark earth; by night Bahloo, the Moon god, sailed serenely across the darkened sky.

The wishes that had been transformed to thought and the thought to action should have brought pleasure to the heart of the Great Spirit, but when dark clouds were torn by lightning and the wind blew chill and fierce down the mountain gorges, sweeping like a scythe through the riotous vegetation, Baiame was aware of the dark thoughts of Marmoo, the Spirit of Evil, the antithesis of all that was good.

And with good reason. Marmoo was talking to his wife, the flame of jealousy hot within him.

'Pride,' he said fiercely. 'Baiame sits there, remote in the sky world, preening himself on his cleverness, because he has created a world full of living things. It's rough and unkempt and no credit to him. I could have made such a world in half the time and to much better effect.'

'Then why didn't you?' the spirit woman asked. There was little love between her and her husband. 'If you are so clever, why don't you make a world? Then I shall believe that you are as powerful as Baiame.'

'It is easy to build something out of nothing,' Marmoo said, 'but more difficult to destroy, once it is there. That is my task.'

Seeing the look on his wife's face, he said harshly, 'Keep watch. I shall begin from this moment,' and strode away without another word.

Working in secret, he fashioned the tribe of insects, ugly as himself in their nature. Some were beautiful to look at, but with poisonous stings, others harmless but capable of walking, crawling, burrowing, or flying. There are some who say that it was Yhi who brought life to the animal and insect creation of Baiame; but there are others who believe that after Marmoo had used his evil imagination to create insects, he breathed life into them and sent them out of the cave where he had hidden them, out of sight of Baiame and Yhi, in vast swarms. The sky was dark with flying insects, the ground a heaving mass of crawling and burrowing grubs, worms, and beetles.

The grass was eaten down to the bare earth. Flowers collapsed, their petals falling like raindrops. Fruit tumbled from the trees and was devoured by the hungry hordes. The music of streams and waterfalls was drowned by the buzzing of wings, the hiss of fighting insects, the clicking of mandibles, as the army flowed on, leaving a trail of desolation.

Looking down on the world, Baiame was dismayed to see the steadily advancing tide of destruction, aware that his enemy had taken this method of challenging his authority. Confident in his own power, he sent one of his winds roaring across the land, hoping to sweep the insects into the sea. It was too late. The hordes of Marmoo were well fed and prepared for anything that Baiame might do. Some burrowed under the earth. Others took refuge in caves or under stones, while the winged destroyers clung to the bark of the trees they had killed. There they waited patiently for the wind to die away, as every wind must some time do, before resuming their march of devastation.

There was only one thing left to do. Baiame came to earth to enlist the aid of good spirits he had left on earth to guide its inhabitants. He travelled quickly to Nungeena, the pleasing spirit who lived in a waterfall in a secluded valley. Even here, Baiame was dismayed to observe, the pleasant dells were dry and bare, every vestige of plant life devoured, the stream choked with the dead bodies of insects that had gorged themselves and lost their footing. The army had passed on, but the smell of death lay heavy in the valley.

'Come with me,' the All-Father said. 'You can see what the insects have done to your pleasant home. The evil tide sent by Marmoo rolls on. Soon there will be no living creature left and the world will be bare and desolate.'

Nungeena called to her attendant spirits, who came from far and near at her bidding.

'What have you seen?' she asked.

They had a sad story to tell of the ravages of Marmoo's brood. Not one part of their domain had been spared, and still the tide rolled on. When they had finished Nungeena, the Mother Spirit, smiled.

'We shall overcome!' she said confidently. 'Look, Father Baiame. The flowers are not all lost. Some I have kept in the shelter of the fall as it cascades over the cliff. None of Marmoo's little people dared come too close to me, and so I was able to preserve them.'

While she was speaking her fingers were at work, deftly weaving the long stalks into a pleasing pattern.

'There!' she said at last with a sigh of satisfaction, setting the beautiful flower arrangement gently on the ground.

Baiame exclaimed with delight.

'The most beautiful of all birds!' he said, and breathed life into a lyre-bird, which spread his plumage and strutted proudly before him. Then the Great Spirit's brow clouded. 'But it doesn't solve the problem of saving our world,' he said gently.

'But that is why I made it,' Nungeena said wonderingly. 'Look.'

As she spoke the bird began scratching among the dry leaves and twigs and rubbish left behind by the insect plague, searching for any that might have been left behind.

'I see,' Baiame said thoughtfully. 'We must make more of them, many more,' and with the deftness of one who had created so many of the wonders of nature, he fashioned birds that flew from his hands as they were completed, and sped in pursuit of the now distant army of insects.

Nungeena followed his example. The attendant spirits, who were much younger, tried to imitate them. They lacked the skill of the older god and goddess, producing butcher-birds and magpies which had little of the grace of other birds, but were equally effective as insect destroyers. The spirits who came from the watery regions made birds that could swim or wade in swamps and rivers. The spirits of coastal lands made gulls who delayed satisfying their appetites with fish while they gorged themselves on insects. The night spirits, whose task was to close the flowers as daylight faded, made mopokes and nightjars. There were birds swift in flight, fantails, and swallows and fly-catchers. The sound of snapping beaks and beating wings rose above the hum of insects as they were caught in flight.

'They are so beautiful they should have voices to match,' Baiame said, and gave them the gift of song. But their sweet music was drowned by the harsh cry of the crows and the raucous laughter of the kookaburras.

The few survivors of the army of Marmoo had been routed. Still singing, the birds circled round Baiame and the guardian spirits, and then flew away in search of other predators that might denude the earth of its vegetation.

26

Never since then have they been so well fed, but they still hope that Marmoo will some day send them another bounteous feast.

Baiame and the Bora Ceremony

As the tribes assembled at Googoorewon, the Place of Trees, Baiame had chosen to disguise himself as a wirinun or medicine-man. It was the first gathering of the men who had sprung from the loins of the first man in honour of the All-Father. Wahn, Du-mer, Biamul, Madhi and many another tribe had gathered from far and near.

Baiame, unrecognised in his disguise, said little. There was much to sadden him, for many of the people were arrogant and others quarrelsome; and much to gladden him, for it was at his command that they had gathered together to celebrate the first initiation ceremony ever held. The young men were undergoing tests before the final combined ceremony in the bora ring that was now being constructed.

For months the young men had been required to support themselves by hunting and eating alone, culminating in a hunt lasting several days, during which no food could be eaten, and then to watch the cooking of the meal they had provided but were not allowed to partake. Severe pain had been inflicted on them, pain they forced themselves to endure without fear. The ordeals imposed alone and in silence had come to an end.

In contrast to what was happening in the bush, there was a constant buzz of activity coming from the ground chosen for the bora circle, sacred designs being painted with clay, with feathers sprinkled over them. tjurunga and other objects had been arranged in their proper places. Baiame watched from a distance with a smile of approval on his face, for the circle was a symbol or representation of the Sky-world from which he came.

The smile was succeeded by a frown. Men of the Madhi tribe were making too much noise, shouting and laughing, taunting the workers, while their women were edging too close to the sacred enclosure. A wirinun ordered them to be quiet and respect the preparations being made for this important ceremony.

'The Great Spirit will be watching you,' he warned them, little knowing that the Great Spirit was standing beside him. The Madhi laughed contemptuously, and behaved more insultingly than before.

The time for punishment had come, Baiame decided, determined that his people should be protected, and the initiates taken safely through their final ordeal. He stepped forward and spoke softly—yet his voice drowned the shouts of the Madhi, seeming to penetrate every corner of the encampment. The men and women were drawn inexorably towards him. Some tried to resist, digging their heels in the ground or holding on to trees, but their efforts were in vain. Feet were dragged through the ground leaving channels in the dust, hands relentlessly torn from trees and rocks. Presently Baiame was surrounded by a silent ring of men and women. Even the Madhi had quietened down, waiting to hear what the strange wirinun had to say.

'I am grieved at your behaviour,' Baiame said. 'My people are happy only because they obey the laws I have laid down from the foundations of the world. Their sacredness must not be violated nor must any of my creation be taken lightly—as it has been by the Madhi during this gathering of the tribes. I have walked in your midst and your behaviour has pleased me. Except for you, the Madhi,' he added sternly, looking at them with eyes that seemed to pierce through their skulls.

The legs of the strongest men trembled at the words of power, as realisation swept through the circle that it was the greatest of all wirinuns who was speaking—the Great Spirit himself. He addressed himself directly to the Madhi.

'You are the ones who have desecrated the bora ground with your shouting and laughter. I can see that this is your nature and nothing will change you. You are not fit to be men. Though it grieves me, I will suffer you, but not as men. In a changed form you may shout and snarl as much as you wish.'

He stretched out his arms. The Madhi fell on all fours before him, as though in supplication. Their legs and arms grew thin, their bodies became covered with coarse hair. No longer could they shout or laugh. The words they tried to utter were distorted in a medley of barks and yelps and snarls. The tails that had sprouted from their bodies curled under them, and they fled from the circle. The men and women of the Madhi tribe would no longer be admitted to the sacred circle, but kept at a distance by stones and sticks. As dingoes they still snarl at the men and women from whom they are descended.

Men still talk in whispers of the first and greatest bora ceremony that was attended by the All-Father in the form of a man. He is with them as a living presence wherever the initiation rites are performed; but only this once, at the first and greatest ceremony of all, did he show himself to them.

Through the nights of spring the singing, the telling, the whispering, the ghostly voices of the tjurunga went on, day and night. While the women waited and wondered, the young men endured the torture of their initiation. The wirinuns moved among them, knocking out their front teeth with stones, wielding knives to cut their flesh. Youth was flowering in the grim ceremony, for where boys had lain down, there arose a new race of men with eyes gleaming and heads held high to face the world in the pride of manhood.

The words of the All-Father rang in their ears: 'You are to be strong, to father sons, to care for your women. You have overcome appetite and pain and fear. You have learned the flight of the honey bee to its store, the water that is hidden in the earth, the trail of the kangaroo-rat over stony ground. Your arms have become strong. The flight of boomerang and the spear that goes from your woomera is swift and true. Your legs will not tire in the chase. Now you must learn the wisdom that has been given to your people, the lore of the stars that turn and circle in my home in the heavens, of winds that blow, and the mystery of air and water. These are the gifts of Baiame that time can never take from you.'

The sound of the tjurungas died away.

'Now you are men,' Baiame said. 'The women have begun the long journey to your tribal hunting grounds. You must follow them as I return to my camping ground, where none of you may venture.'

And so the Great Spirit who had appeared to his people as a wirinun vanished from their sight. Behind the mask of that calm mortal face there was sadness, for the Father Spirit knew that sorrow and pain as well as joy had been born into his world at the first bora.

But Baiame is wise with wisdom beyond that of men. He knew that good can come from evil, that knowledge is born of suffering, and understanding is the child of experience.

Baiame and the Flying Grinding Stones

AT the first corroboree there were lighter moments. In the form of a wirinun the All-Father had wandered through the great encampment, savouring the moments of peace and the little problems and difficulties that men and women strove so valiantly to overcome. If such a thing can be said of one who was the source of all things, Baiame had enough of mankind in him to relish the humour that underlies the efforts of struggling men and women.

One morning, while strolling through the encampment, he came across a group of women who were looking puzzled and downcast.

'What is your trouble?' he asked. 'Why are you not at work?'

'Oh sir,' one of them replied, her companions being too overcome to speak to the all-powerful wirinun, 'do not think we are idle. We gathered here, where we had left the stones last night, so we could grind a supply of grass seed ready for a meal tonight. But we can't find them. They have left us.'

Hiding a smile, Baiame said, 'That is surely a strange thing. I have heard of women leaving their grinding stones, but never before has anyone told me that it is the grinding stone that has gone away. What do you think has happened? Have your stones sprouted wings with which to fly?'

The woman defended herself.

'We did not leave them,' she maintained. 'We hid them in a safe place where no one could find them. When we came to get them they were gone.'

'Certainly they are not here,' Baiame admitted, 'but it may be your hiding place was not as secure as you thought. Or perhaps you have forgotten that you lent them to someone. Who is camped next to you?'

'The Du-mers,' she said.

'Then you had better ask them if they've seen them.'

The women were quite sure that the Du-mers had not taken them but, remembering the fate of the Madhi, it seemed unwise to argue with Baiame. Some went to the Du-mer, others scattered in various directions, asking tribe after tribe whether they had seen any grinding stones. The reply was always the same: 'No. The ones we have here belong to us.'

While the women were engaged in their search, Baiame heard an unusual drumming sound. He looked up and saw a Wunda, a spirit that is invisible to human eyes, flying at tree-top level towards the camping place of the Du-mer.

He stroked his beard and said to himself, 'Oh, I may have done those women an injustice!'

Lifting his voice, he called them to him and said, 'Follow me. I'll show you something you have never seen before.'

He led them to the edge of the bush where they could see across a bare plain. To their astonishment, there were the grinding stones, each one flying a few metres above the ground, apparently without support of any kind.

'You were quite right,' Baiame said to the woman who had dared to speak to him. 'They really are leaving you. Don't look so surprised. They are being carried away by the Wunda spirits. I know you can't see them, but each of them is carrying one of your grinding stones. Watch what happens next.'

As he was speaking, the women of the Du-mer tribe came running out of the bush, racing swiftly after the flying grinding stones. The leading woman had nearly touched the last of the stones when Baiame stretched out his arms. In a flash all the Du-mer women were turned into Brown Pigeons. Flapping their wings, they soared into the air and continued the chase.

'See if you can catch them!' Baiame shouted. The women who had lost their stones chased the Du-mers, and the Du-mers chased the Wundas. Baiame sauntered after them, laughing to himself at the sight of the fleeing stones, the Brown Pigeons, and the throng of women following them.

The Wundas began to tire. As their pursuers caught up with them, they dropped their burdens and flew away. The Du-mers gave up the chase and winged their way back to their encampment. Only the women were left, looking at a mountain

31

that had suddenly reared itself above the level plain—a mountain composed entirely of grinding stones.

It was given the name Dirangiburra, and to this day, tribes that want the best grinding stones go to the mountain to secure them.

The Wives of Baiame

BAIAME spent a long period of time in the world he had created, much of it on the summit of Mount Oobi-oobi, a peak in Bullima. While there, he took two wives, Birra-nulu and Kunnan-beili, who proved something of a trial to him. The wisdom of the Great Spirit must surely have been asleep when he chose women who were so young and addle-brained. Much of his time was spent in keeping them in order and seeing they did not get into mischief.

One day he told them of his intention to go hunting, and gave strict instructions on what to do while he was away.

'I want you to dig some yams and find as many frogs as you can. Don't forget to take your digging sticks with you. When you have gathered as many as you need for a meal, take them to the spring at Coorigil and wait for me there.

'Now listen carefully. No matter how hot or tired you may be, you must not bathe in the spring. That's an order. I have filled the pool with water for drinking. No one must ever bathe in it.'

This he said, not because of the pretended prohibition against bathing, but because of the dangers he knew lurked in the pool.

Before he was out of sight the young women took their digging sticks and went to a spot where they knew there were plenty of yams. Then they went on to the ponds and, long before midday, their dilly-bags were filled with yams and frogs. It was a long trek to the spring at Coorigil where they were to camp that night. They threw their burdens on the ground, found a mossy patch on which to lie, and were soon sound asleep.

The sun was still high above their heads when they woke.

'I'm hot,' Kunnan-beili said. 'I expect old Baiame's found a shady tree, leaving us to swelter in the sun.'

Birra-nulu agreed.

'I don't see why he couldn't have let us go to a cool, shady place while we're waiting. The water looks very refreshing, doesn't it?'

Kunnan-beili agreed.

'If he had told us it was good for swimming but that we mustn't drink the water, I'd have understood. He didn't say that, did he?'

'No. He said we could drink it but we mustn't bathe in it. Sounds silly, doesn't it? I wonder what he's getting at?'

'I know,' Kunnan-beili said. 'He doesn't like swimming. He knows we do, so he's just being selfish. Nothing could happen to us if we took one little dip, could it?'

There was no need for an answer to that question. Unhampered by clothes, they jumped straight into the pool, splashing each other and shrieking with delight. The fact that it had been forbidden by their husband added to their enjoyment.

Their frolics lasted a very short while. Hidden in the depths of the pool two huge crocodiles, the Kurria guardians, felt the unusual turbulence of the water. Opening their eyes, they saw bubbles and wavelets far above them. Swimming silently upwards, they opened their jaws to their fullest extent, and swallowed the girls whole.

The song of birds ceased abruptly, the breeze died away, animals gazed in horror at the eddies on the surface of the water and the grim shapes that vanished in the depths of the pool.

The Kurrias eyed each other apprehensively. Their bellies were full, but in their sluggish minds was the uneasy thought that the women they had swallowed were the wives of Baiame, of Baiame who had made them and who, at a word or even a thought, could unmake them. In their greed they had forfeited their role as guardians of the pool. When Baiame learned what they had done, it would be difficult to escape his vengeance. The same thought slowly percolated through their minds. The pool that had been their home was no longer a safe place. Fortunately they knew of a hidden escape route. Near the bottom were two apertures large enough to take even their swollen bodies. One brought water to the pool. It was of no use now, for the stream came from the hills, springing from a tiny rivulet far up on a stony hillside. The other, larger channel led to the Narran River. The crocodiles squeezed through the opening and struggled along the underground stream. Normally they would never have essayed such a dangerous journey. Now it was doubly trying, for their distended bellies scraped against rocks. Bends in the channel had to be negotiated carefully. Twisting their bodies, they eased themselves round the many obstructions. Speed was necessary lest Baiame should surprise them when they were unable to use their tails.

They had not emerged from the tunnel when Baiame arrived at the spring. Seeing no sign of his wives, he thought at first that they might not have arrived at the rendezvous. Throwing down the wallaby he had caught, he lay down to rest. His head had barely touched the ground when he noticed two digging sticks leaning against a rock. On top of them were two dilly-bags that squirmed and wriggled, threatening to crash to the ground below. He sat up. These were the yamsticks and the bags that belonged to his wives, the bags doubtless filled with live frogs.

'The Kurrias!' he exclaimed, realising that his wives must have disobeyed his order, and been carried away by the Kurrias. Fearing for their lives, he peered into the pool. All he could see was disturbed water—no wives, no Kurria guardians. Bending his head until it was under water, he could discern the black cavities in the walls of the pool. Realising that there could only be one reason for them to desert their post, he knew that they would be moving slowly, dragged down by the weight of Birra-nulu and Kunnan-beili.

Hurrying across country, he scuffed the land into the ridges that lead towards the Narran River. His footsteps took him to a part of the river where it spread out into a shallow lake. There he sat and waited for the Kurrias to appear. As soon as their snouts poked through the channel exit he sprang to his feet, fitted a spear to his woomera and pierced one of them through the head, pinning it to the lake bed. The second one, emerging more cautiously, he stunned with his nulla-nulla.

He drew the crocodiles out of the water, laid them on the bank and, drawing his knife from his girdle, slit their bellies longitudinally.

The bodies of Birra-nulu and Kunnan-beili rolled out and lay still. Baiame bent over them and examined them closely. They were still breathing, though the rise and fall of their breasts was almost imperceptible. From head to foot they were clothed in slime from the bellies of the Kurrias. Leaving them where they lay, their husband searched until he found a nest of red ants which he sprinkled over their bodies. The insects ran across their bodies, through their hair, and into every fold and crevice, licking the slime until it had completely disappeared and their skins shone in the sunlight. Roused by the tickling of many feet and by painful bites in the more tender parts of their anatomy, the young women sat up and climbed shakily to their feet.

'What has happened? Where are we?' they asked, for the last they remembered was sunshine and cool water on their skins before being engulfed in the womb-like darkness and heat of the crocodile stomachs.

Baiame talked to them gently, as one would talk to little children, and they were ashamed of their disobedience.

'Never again will we disobey you,' they said, hanging their heads; and Baiame, so wise yet so foolish in his dealings with young women, smiled at them, and believed they were speaking the truth.

And who shall blame him—for have not the wisest of men been deceived by women, and forgiven them, only to find that their words were like a ripple on the water that dies away as quickly as it comes?

Baiame the Benefactor

THOUGH far removed from the world in his mountain eyrie or the even more remote Sky-land, Baiame had a perpetual interest in everything that happened here. In extreme cases he interfered in the hope that he might avert the evils that plagued mankind. This was exemplified in the story of Bullai-bullai, Weedah, and Beereeun.

Bullai-bullai was the idol of the clan, desired by the young men, but most of all by Weedah, the most skilled of the hunters. He was the fortunate one, for Bullai-bullai returned his love and looked forward to the day when she would be given to him in marriage.

But alas! Giving and taking in marriage is not the prerogative of young people.

'You are to be the wife of Beereeun,' the young woman was told.

Her heart sank. This was a fate she had feared ever since she had reached puberty. Beereeun was old and ugly, noted for his uncertain temper, and feared even by the old men. For Beereeun was a medicine-man, replete with knowledge gained over many years, crafty and powerful. No secrets were hidden from him, no task beyond his power, no limit to the evil he was able to bring on those who dared confront him.

The marriage day was fast approaching. Concealed in the dense bush that ringed their encampment, Weedah and Bullai-bullai clung to each other, excited yet appalled at the daring plan they had devised. Weedah was to set out on the hunt the next day. It was his usual practice and would not attract attention. Bullai-bullai would go with the other girls to search for yams and witchety grubs. As unobtrusively as possible, she would drift away from the crowd; once out of sight, she was to hurry to a pre-arranged meeting place where Weedah was waiting, and together they would make their way to some far distant region. Where it would be and what it would be like there they could not know but, for good or ill, they would be with each other.

The plan had its drawbacks. Weedah would not be missed until nightfall but it seemed likely that Bullai-bullai's absence would be noted during the afternoon when the women returned to prepare the evening meal. The lovers hoped that she would not be missed until the daylight was too far advanced to permit a search to be made, for the younger and more vigorous men would probably not return to the encampment until night fell.

The best that could happen was for the pursuit to be delayed until the following morning; the worst, that news of Bullai-bullai's disappearance might come to the ears of Beereeun, who would devise a spell to bring a sudden end to their elopement.

On the fateful day, all went well. Bullai-bullai and Weedah met and put a great distance between them and the camp, travelling all day and night until forced to stop for sheer exhaustion. Their departure was not noticed until late in the day, giving the fugitives a clear run.

The hunt was to begin at first light on the following day. No matter how much the young warriors might sympathise with Bullai-bullai, no one dared defy Beereeun by refusing to join in the chase.

The real danger lay not with the warriors, but with the revengeful Beereeun. While remaining in the camp, he recited incantations that put many obstacles in the path of Weedah and Bullai-bullai. During the days that followed, they overcame them one by one, though with increasing difficulty.

When their strength was nearly exhausted they came to a deep, wide, swiftly-flowing river, with no means of crossing it. They were too tired to risk swimming to the far bank, and were in despair, when they saw a small bark canoe being paddled towards them by an old man. Goolay-yali was a peculiar person, with a jaw that was half as big as his canoe. At first he refused to convey them across the river, but soon changed his mind when he saw the look on Weedah's face.

'Yes, I will take you over,' he said, 'but you can see for yourselves that my canoe is too frail to carry three people. It would sink under us and we'd be swept away in the current. Let the man come first and I will return for the woman.'

It was their only hope of putting the river between them and their fellow-tribesmen, who by this time could not be far behind.

With Weedah safely on the far bank Goolay-yali the ferryman returned to where Bullai-bullai was waiting. As she was about to step into the canoe, Goolay-yali pushed her back.

'Stay where you are,' he said roughly. 'I've been without a woman for many years. Do you think I'd let such a fine-looking young woman leave me, now I've got her? Get a fire going while I catch some fish for our meal.'

Bullai-bullai looked despairingly at her lover, who had seen what was happening and was waving frantically to her. There was nothing he could do to save the woman he loved.

With tears streaming down her face Bullai-bullai gathered wood, regarding Goolay-yali with loathing. By the time the fire had died down to glowing embers and ash, the old man gave her fish to cook. In desperation she bent down, scooped up a double handful of white ash, and threw it in his face. Goolay-yali staggered back, howling with pain and rage, rubbing his eyes, and hopping from one foot to another. Bullai-bullai turned to run—and found Beereeun blocking her way with a grim smile on his face.

'So you thought to escape me!' he said, seizing her arm in a painful grip. 'You and your precious Weedah have sadly underestimated my powers. Now you will pay for running away from your promised husband.'

Still holding her in a painful grip, he looked across the river to where the frantic hunter was fitting a spear to his woomera in the vain hope of killing the wirinun. Extending his right arm Beereeun chanted secret words in a high-pitched, unnatural voice. A bolt of lightning seemed to flash from his extended fingers, linking him with Weedah. It lasted only as long as the blinking of an eye, and then there was no sign of Weedah save for his weapons that lay in an untidy heap on the river bank.

'Where is he? What have you done to him?' Bullai-bullai cried in anguish.

'I have done you a great favour,' the wirinun replied. 'If you had both escaped, the years would have passed quickly and he would have died. Now you will be able to see him every night.'

He pointed to a certain spot in the sky.

'That is where you will find him—a bright new star I have given to you and to our children in the years to come.'

'What shall I do?' she moaned as the tears ran down her face. 'Turn me into a star, too, that I may be with him.'

Beereeun grinned.

'No. I have other plans. You are my woman now, to work and comfort me in my old age and bear me many children. You have been promised to me by your parents and by the old men. All I am doing is to take what is mine.'

He turned her towards him—and at that very moment Baiame, who sees everything, intervened. For a second time there was a flash of lightning, blinding in its intensity—so bright that Bullai-bullai covered her face with her hands. Beereeun and Goolay-yali stumbled into the shelter of nearby rocks and crouched down.

Thunder rolled across hills and plains, shaking the earth; and in the thunder the cowering men and the grief-stricken girl heard the voice of the Great Spirit.

'I can see you, Beereeun,' it said. 'It is fitting that you should crawl in the crevices of the rocks.'

Bullai-bullai peeped through spread fingers. Beereeun was no longer there. In his place was an ugly little lizard whose colour blended with the rocks as he scuttled further into the shelter of the boulders.

Again the voice thundered and re-echoed from the hills.

'Goolay-yali, you who desired a woman who craved mercy from you, the ashes with which you are covered will be the sign of your shame, now and for ever.'

Where he had been standing there was now a white pelican, covered in white feathers, with thin legs and a huge pouch under his beak that resembled the scuttle-like mouth of the man who had been Goolay-yali.

Then the All-Father's voice softened and spoke words of comfort to the young woman who stood alone by the river bank.

'I cannot give you back to Weedah,' he said gently. 'I can create but I cannot turn time backwards. He is happy where he is, looking down at you in wonder, for new beauty has come to you this day, and at night you will be able to look up at him with the eyes of love and see the glory that Beereeun gave him so unwittingly. Now look at yourself, my chosen one, for I have given you robes that will delight your loved one in the heavens, and all men who see you.'

Bullai-bullai looked down and saw that she was indeed clothed in garments brighter and more colourful than any that she had ever seen—a soft and shining array of green and red and white—and was comforted.

So, on that day, the All-Father who loves his children and sees that justice is done, created Bullai-bullai the Parrot, Weedah the star,* Beereeun the Lizard, and Goolay-yali the Pelican.

---

* Weedah is the star we know as Canopus.

The Making of Mankind

How the world began and was populated with animal life is the substance of countless myths in every part of the world. Man has groped his way towards truth in fear of gods and spirits, and pictures it in many anthropomorphic forms. The Australian Aboriginal had a more lofty concept than many other primitive peoples. Tribal versions of the many separate acts of creation varied enormously. This, too, is indicative of their fertility of imagination, for in the Dreamtime few things remained constant. The journey and the dreaming of one totemic ancestor would differ in nearly every respect from that of other ancestors.

In the Centre the primal cause of creation was believed to be the goddess of the sun. Not the sun itself, but the spirit of the sun, the Great Spirit, the Mother, richly endowed and fecund, but yet spirit, whose power was manifested in thought and, through other agencies, in action. According to the wisest men, the agency through which she worked before her departure was one known variously as Baiame, Spirit Father, or All-Father.

Baiame, the male counterpart of the female Yhi, the Sun goddess, was not only her representative, but her alter ego, created by her, partaking of her divinity.* To him she had entrusted the task of forming and caring for animal life in its infinite variety. One thing only was lacking—the form and intelligence of man. This task, too, was entrusted to the Father Spirit. He felt the responsibility keenly and determined to proceed cautiously by injecting the superior element into his charges.

The first experiments were unsuccessful. The characteristics of men and women of the future resulted only in dissatisfaction. Kangaroos grew ashamed of their tails, not realising that without them they would lose speed and mobility. Fish became

---

* The myth of the creation of animals and subsequently of mankind is related in W. Ramsay Smith, *Myths and Legends of the Australian Aboriginals* (George G. Harrap & Co.). Although the present retelling is based on Ramsay Smith's account, one cannot avoid the impression that it is, to say the least, coloured by western thought.

impatient of their confinement to water, birds craved the loss of wings in return for the agility of kangaroos, insects demanded an increase in size. It was a time of change and turmoil, but Baiame remained calm, knowing that his decision had been approved by the goddess.

'It is part of the birth pangs of creation,' Yhi assured him. 'Until the form of man can be decided, we can only experiment with these creations, observing the changes and the effect on their habits.'

When at last the experiments were complete, Baiame gathered birds, animals, and insects together in a huge cave. Baiame and Yhi acted in concert, plucking what may be described as the incubated fragments of the spirit of man from their animal hosts, amalgamating them into one cohesive whole. The animal creation looked on in astonishment. The longings and aspirations that belong to man alone were lost to them for ever. Content with their true nature, they streamed out of the cave. As they went, man, newly fashioned and imbued with longings, desires, pride, endurance and a portion of the Great Spirit that had fashioned him from the animals, watched them as they ran and flew towards their natural environment. He alone of all creation was master of the inheritance bestowed on him by the All-Father.

Baiame, Punjel, and Kookaburra

ALTHOUGH the Great Spirit is known by several names amongst tribal groups, in a legend that tells how Baiame and Punjel inhabited the Milky Way, Punjel is regarded as a Father Spirit, yet subordinate to Baiame.

At the time the story begins Baiame had not yet decided on the final form and size of animals. Darkness still covered the earth. His first experiments resulted in the creation of monstrous birds and animals. In the dim light of the stars, the huge, half-formed creatures roamed over the world like moving mountains, in the hopeless search for sufficient food to sustain their misshapen bodies. In consequence there was ceaseless fighting and quarrelling over the meagre supply of food.

The noise of battle between birds and animals gave little peace to the gods of the Milky Way, who themselves were dissatisfied with their conditions. It was bitterly cold in the immense expanse of the heavens. Much of their time was spent in gathering firewood in the expectation of kindling a fire to keep themselves warm. Punjel did most of the work. As the heap of firewood grew, he begged Baiame to provide the much needed fire.

'Fire must first come from the earth,' the Supreme Spirit informed him. 'Not yet does it exist.'

'Then why don't you hurry and make it?' Punjel asked peevishly.

'The work of creation must not be hurried,' Baiame replied solemnly. 'Do you not see that if I were to finalise my work too soon, the birds and animals I am working on would remain as they are now, a menace to a world that must be well ordered if it is to be worthy of us. There are natural processes at work there. In due time you will find all your problems solved, Punjel—and that time is not far distant.'

Time went by. The pile of firewood grew to an enormous size, and still Baiame and Punjel were cold. There was no sign of the promised fire. Punjel grew impatient. He peered down, straining his eyes in the hope of seeing a flicker of light that would indicate that fire had come into the world. With eyes accustomed to the gloom, all he could see was the turbulence of gigantic bodies fighting over the supply of food. He saw Kangaroo and Wombat striking each other with their paws, and Eagle-hawk and Emu fighting over the carcase of a dead animal. His attention was attracted to the two birds.

Emu snatched the body away from Eagle-hawk and, with legs like tree trunks, raced across a vast plain. Eagle-hawk went in hot pursuit, pulling feathers from the tail of the larger bird. Emu continued her flight, still holding the carcase in her beak, leading Eagle-hawk away from her nest, where Punjel could see several eggs glimmering in the faint light.

Eagle-hawk gave up the chase. He wandered back and stumbled over the nest. Punjel expected he would break the eggs and eat them, but the inchoate monster had not yet learnt to recognise eggs as a source of food. He picked up one of the eggs, transferred it to his claw, and hurled it up to the sky.

The egg smashed against Punjel's wood pile, where it burst into flame. The sky and the world were lit by the brilliant white and gold of Emu's egg. The timber that Punjel had gathered so laboriously caught fire and burned with a steady flame. The black night fled, the stars vanished, heat flamed on the faces and bodies of the gods, and the cold of the empty sky was swallowed up in the comforting warmth of that primal fire.

Once their limbs were warm, the gods looked down at the world Baiame had made. Punjel was astonished. Never had he dreamed that such beauty could exist. Where before he had seen nothing but dark, amorphous mountains and moving forms, now there were snow-capped peaks, hills that had thrust themselves above flowering plains, rivers winding their way through valleys and plains until they reached the encircling seas. Gone were the lumbering bodies of the dinosaurian monsters, dwindled to such an extent that the smaller ones were invisible even to the eyes of the gods.

Punjel was overcome.

'I did not know that you were working in the darkness,' he confessed. 'Now we can enjoy it for ever.'

'Not for us alone,' Baiame reminded him. 'The animals have found their true nature, in shape and in size, but there are even smaller scraps left over that must be transformed into insects and fish. Last of all, we must make men and women, to enjoy what has been made.'

'The fire is dying,' Punjel said. 'Look, shadows are creeping back. All this beauty will vanish when the blackness returns and we shall be as cold as we have ever been.'

'No, cold and darkness there will be, to remind the world of times that were, but even they will be a benison—cold to refresh bodies that are burned in the heat of the day, darkness to provide a setting for the myriad stars of our own Sky-land. We shall divide time into night when all is dark, and day in which it is light.'

'Where will the light come from when the fire is out?' Punjel asked. 'This night of which you speak is with us once more. Even the embers are dying and the cold is creeping back. I can feel it.'

Baiame smiled. 'You will gather more wood each night, Punjel. That is your task, a noble task for a god.'

'But who will light the fire?'

'Fire is with us now. Each morning I shall touch the wood you have gathered, and light and heat will return—and men will call it Yhi, the goddess of the sun.'

'What will the birds and animals and reptiles and insects and fish you have created do when the darkness comes?'

'They will sleep through the hours of darkness.'

'What is sleep?'

'Sleep is a kind of not-living. A time when they lie still with eyes closed, to repair the ravages of the day and let life run through tired bodies in preparation for a new day.'

Punjel was still puzzled.

'I can understand this state of being not-alive, not-dead,' he said, 'but how will they come to full life again when their eyes are closed and they are only half alive?'

'I shall hang a bright star in the sky, to tell them it is time to wake.'

'But their eyes will be closed.'

'Then there must be a noise to waken them so they may know it is time to open their eyes,' Baiame said impatiently.

'Who will make the noise that wakens men and animals?'

'That I leave to you, Punjel. You must find a way to make a noise that will waken the sleeping world each new morning.'

As Punjel gathered fresh wood through the night that had closed in on him again, he thought of the problem Baiame had set, but could find no solution. When the wood pile was set alight he descended to the world and wandered through the bush beside a murmuring stream. He listened for sounds he hoped might wake the sleeping animals—the creaking of branches in the wind, the voice of flowing water, and a distant growl of thunder, but not one of these was sufficient for his purpose.

Suddenly the animals opened their eyes and jumped to their feet. The startled birds flapped their wings and flew out of the trees. Punjel froze where he stood. The air was rent by raucous laughter. Looking up, he saw Kookaburra, the only one of all creation who had been woken by the kindling of the fire. He was perched on a branch, clattering his bill. He had laughed at the sight of the sleeping animals, and was now enjoying the joke of seeing them woken by the noise he had made.

44

'Kookaburra!' Punjel exclaimed. 'You have solved my problem! Can you laugh louder still?'

Kookaburra clattered his beak again and released such a peal of laughter that Punjel was forced to block his ears with his hands.

'Enough!' he cried. 'Tell me, Kookaburra, are you prepared to be the sentinel of the morning for Baiame and myself? Before the Great Spirit lights the fire I prepare each morning, he will hang a star in the eastern sky as a warning to men and animals that dawn has come, but he fears they will not wake to see it. Will you watch for it and when the fire is lit, wake the world with your laughter?'

Kookaburra had no words with which to reply but again chattered and laughed, and Punjel knew he had the answer he sought.

'Have you performed the task I gave you?' Baiame asked when Punjel returned to the Sky-land.

Punjel smiled and said, 'Wait until tomorrow!'

When tomorrow came, Baiame was startled by the ringing peal of laughter that could be heard even among the paling stars. It was the voice of Kookaburra, the voice that greets every new morning with laughter.

Bunjil

ANOTHER Great Spirit, or the same Great Spirit with the name Bunjil, was the creative entity in the myths of the Kulin people of central Victoria. Aldo Massola, who collected the myths and legends of this and other tribes in his book *Bunjil's Cave*, records that Bunjil was 'headman' of the Kulin, and that he possessed two wives and a son named Binbeal. Binbeal was the Rainbow, his wife being the fainter bow that sometimes appears at the same time.

Bunjil performed his creative function while on earth. He was assisted by six wirinuns, all of whom were young and vigorous. They were Djurt-djurt the Kestrel, Thara the Quail Hawk, Yukope the Parrakeet, Dantum the Parrot, Tadjeri the Brush-tail Possum, and Turnung the Glider Possum.

The following tales have been selected to demonstrate the creature activities of Bunjil while he remained in the world of men, and the reason for his final departure to the Sky-land.

Bunjil the Creator

BUNJIL, like Baiame, was not satisfied until he had created sentient human beings. It was a harder task than any he had attempted. The making of other forms of animal life had been comparatively simple. The making of a man was a challenge to the Great Spirit, for within the framework of flesh there was need for powers of thought, reasoning, and other human characteristics that would separate man from the animal creation.

He pondered long before attempting the supreme masterpiece. When at last he was ready he prepared two sheets of bark, cutting them to the shape he envisaged as suited to such a noble purpose. Mobility and dexterity were important, and these he incorporated into his design. Next he took soft clay, moulding it to the shape of the bark, smoothing it with his hands.

When the work was finished he danced round the two inert figures, implanting seeds of knowledge and the capacity to reason and learn.

The time had come for his skill to be put to the test. He gave them names—Berrook-boorn and Kookin-berrook. This was the first and most important step, for without names they would have lacked personality and spirit. Bunjil was well aware that if these beings were to fulfil their purpose, they must share his spirit as well as the characteristics of animals.

Although without breath they were now named and ready for the infilling of the life force. Again Bunjil danced round them and then lay on their bodies, one after the other, breathing breath and life into their mouths, nostrils, and navels.

For the third time Bunjil danced round them. As his feet wove intricate patterns in the dust, Berrook-boorn and Kookin-berrook rose slowly to their feet. They linked hands with Bunjil and with each other, joining the All-Father in the dance of life, singing with him the first song that ever came from the lips of man.

In another myth the creation of woman was less romantic than that of men.

Balayang* the Bat was enjoying himself paddling in the shallow water at the edge of the Goulburn River, scooping it up with his hands, and splashing it in the air. The mud at the river bottom was stirred up until he could no longer see through it. Tiring of this, he stripped the leaves from a fallen branch and poked it into the mud. Presently he felt something soft and yielding, yet heavier and more solid than the mud in which it was resting.

Curious to know what it could be, he poked it with the stick and felt it roll over but, try as he might, he was unable to bring it to the surface. Withdrawing the stick, he bent it into a hook and succeeded in catching the mysterious object.

When it emerged he saw two hands, a head, a body, and two feet. It was the body of a woman. As he was dragging it on to the bank, two more hands appeared. A second body had broken loose and was floating to the surface.

Wondering what he had discovered, for never before had Balayang seen a woman, he took the bodies to Bunjil and laid them at his feet.

'These are women,' the Great Spirit said. 'They are made to be companions and helpers of men. This is Kunnawarra, the Black Swan, and this one Kururuk, the Native Companion.'

As he spoke, men gathered round him, anxious to see the first women. Bunjil held his hands over them and gave them life. The women stood up, looking at the men who encircled them and then at the Great Spirit.

'You are to live with the men,' he said. 'Man is not complete without you, nor will you be complete without him.'

He gave each a digging stick, symbolic of their destiny as gatherers of vegetable food, and to the men spears and spear-throwers, as a sign that they were to be hunters of animals and protectors of their womenfolk.

---

* Also spelt Pally-yan.

The emergence of mankind, male and female, was the crowning achievement of the All-Father, but his work was not confined to this, nor to the creation of animal life. There is a homely tale of how the Great Spirit went hunting with his six trusty wirinuns and a number of other men at what is now Port Phillip in Victoria, which was then a wide plain. While they were away, and their wives engaged in collecting food for the evening meal, only a few old women and children remained in the camp.

The women were so immersed in camp gossip that they failed to notice what the children were doing. An argument had arisen and the boys had taken sides. Blows were exchanged and, in the midst of the excitement, a dish of water was upset. If it had been an ordinary coolamon, no harm would have been done but, as it happened, it was the one that belonged to Bunjil and of course possessed magic properties.

When it was knocked over, the contents were spilt, but that was only the beginning. A never-ending torrent poured out of the dish, flooding the encampment and spreading across the plain. At first the water was shallow, but as the stream continued to gush over the side of the dish, it rose, inundating the hills and threatening a much wider area.

Bunjil had been mildly surprised when he first noticed the tide of water at his feet. As it grew deeper, and his men found themselves waist-deep in the water, he realised that he must act quickly if he were to save the newly-made world from destruction.

Plucking two huge rocks from a nearby hill, he threw them on to the ground. They fell on the edge of the creeping waters, not far from each other. He ordered the stream to flow between them and lose itself in the ocean. He was just in time. The waters remained where they were, ebbing and flowing between the rocks that guard the entrance to Port Phillip.

Bunjil's work was nearing an end. The land was fair, adorned with vegetation ranging from moss and tiny blades of grass to the tall trees that stood stiff and unyielding in the still air. Animal life was abundant and infinite in variety, flying, scurrying across the ground, and burrowing through the soil. Only the trees and plants remained motionless, as though Bunjil had forgotten to give them life.

'There must be movement, for life is a pulsating state of ceaseless activity,' he murmured. 'There must be moving air to carry the clouds on its back, strong winds to bend the trees, and fitful breezes to enable birds to fight against them and make them strong.'

He looked round him. Bellin-bellin the Crow was behind him, with an airtight bag suspended from his neck.

'Have you kept the winds I gave you to mind safe in your bag?' he asked.

'Yes, Great Father Bunjil, they are all there. Not one has escaped.'

'Good! Now you may open it and release some of the winds.'

Bellin-bellin cautiously opened one corner of the bag. A gentle breeze sped across the western lands, another to the east, another to the south, and a fiercer, colder wind to the north.

The trees waved their branches, the birds lifted their voices as they felt the fresh air caressing their bodies, and even the insects and lizards joined in praise of Bunjil, the Great Provider.

'That is good,' Bunjil told him. 'One last wind, please, a stronger one, a colder one, that will challenge my children to be brave and stand up to raging storms, and prepare them for the evil years that may lie ahead.'

Bellin-bellin opened the neck of the bag wider still, and out roared a screaming wind with snow and the chill of high mountain pools, cold and bracing.

'Enough! Enough!' cried Bunjil. 'No one can withstand the power of the south wind.'

So strong was that wind that it bent the tall trees double and denuded them of their leaves, while he and his family were blown right out of the world, together with all their possessions. It did not stop blowing until Bunjil and all his relatives and followers were blown back to their permanent home in the sky.

Bunjil and his People

BUNJIL'S six young wirinuns had caught a kangaroo and were preparing it for a meal when Berrimun came up to them and screwed up his face as though in pain.

49

'What's the matter with you?' the wirinuns asked.

'My teeth are sore,' Berrimun said, pretending the pain was excruciating.

'What a pity,' they said. 'We were about to offer you some of our meat, but if your teeth are sore, it won't be of any use to you.'

'No, that is so,' Berrimun said, 'but if you let me suck a little of its blood before you put it on the fire, it might do me good.'

'Very well,' they said.

Berrimun sank his teeth into the flesh and sucked so hard that he drained it of every drop of blood, leaving the meat dry and tasteless.

Bunjil had been watching the performance, and was well aware of the trick Berrimun had played on his young men.

'He must pay for this,' he said, and gave them permission to punish him. They clubbed him with their nulla-nullas, knocking out his teeth, which stuck to his chin, and there they remain as spines on the chins of the Berrimun, the Bloodsucker Lizards.

Besides punishing those who deserved it, Bunjil was ready to help those who were in need. These traits in his character were exemplified in his treatment of Karwine the Crane.

Karwine's wife came to the Great Spirit one day with a complaint that she was being ill-treated by her husband.

'Tell me what he does to you,' Bunjil asked.

'He beats me when I have done no wrong. I have been a good wife to him, but he has no love for me. This very day he brought back some possums. I cooked them for him. He ate them, but wouldn't give me any.'

When Bunjil was sure the woman was telling the truth, he sought out the vicious Crane and threw his spear at it. Karwine saw it coming and flew away. The spear struck his knees, preventing him from drawing up his legs; and that is why cranes fly with their legs stretched out instead of being drawn up to their bodies.

In spite of the care that Bunjil showed for his people, it was important not to offend him—a lesson that Balayang learned to his cost. Bunjil had chosen to live close to the Yarra River, a region for which he had much affection; Balayang the Bat was equally fond of the home he had made for himself in a dark cave on a mountain side. It was festooned with plants, damp and cool inside, and well protected from predators. Bunjil felt sorry that Balayang was forced to remain in what he regarded as dank, gloomy, and unpleasant surroundings and invited him to join him on the pleasant meadows by the riverside.

Balayang knew very well that Bunjil's pleasant meadows were no place for him, and imagined that the Great Spirit was slighting him on account of his choice of a home. Without thinking of the consequences, he sent a reply that said simply: 'I have chosen my home because it is the best. I invite you to come and live with me.'

Bunjil was annoyed by this curt reception of his invitation. Calling Djurt-djurt and Thara to him, he told them to set fire to the country of which Balayang had taken possession. The wirinuns did as they were commanded, but had much difficulty in setting the damp mountainside bush alight. The only damage suffered by the Bat was from the smoke that poured into the cave, covering him with soot and ash, turning his skin black.

Nurunderi

ANOTHER name for the Great Spirit was Nepelle who, in South Australian myth, is almost overshadowed by his messenger Nurunderi, who suffered the tribulations that lesser men so often have with their wives.

His activities, which included the formation of the Murray River, were not confined to South Australia. His home in the world of Nepelle's making was between Lakes Albert and Alexandrina. His initial reception was disappointing, for many of the tribesmen were so frightened of him that they hid in the scrub. When they refused to respond to his demands, he felt they were unworthy of Nepelle's trust and changed them into birds.

When, therefore, he was received cordially by the Narrinyeri tribe, he was delighted and made his home amongst them. But, in spite of his wisdom, Nurunderi was too easily beguiled by women. On a hunting expedition as he passed two grass-trees, he heard melancholy voices calling for help.

'Where are you?' he called. 'Can I help you?'

The messenger of the god was always ready to offer assistance to anyone in trouble, for he had spent a long life in the service of the men and women with whom he had been living.

'We are here, shut up in the grass-trees where you are standing,' came the reply.

'What have you done to be punished in this way?' Nurunderi asked.

'We have done nothing wrong,' the female voices said in concert. 'Wicked men have shut us up in the grass-trees. We have to remain here until a good man consents to set us free.'

Nurunderi responded quickly to the plea. The fresh young voices sounded appealingly in his ears. He was old and tired, and it may be that he craved companionship, for in all the years he had spent in the service of Nepelle, he had never experienced the ministrations of women, nor entered into marriage. If only he had made inquiry and checked their story, he would have learnt that the young women of the grass-trees had created so much dissension amongst the tribespeople that they had been kept out of mischief by being confined to a vegetable existence.

Making up his mind on the spur of the moment, he said, 'By the power of the Great Spirit invested in me, I command you to come out and show yourselves as women.'

He was delighted when two nubile girls stood in front of him, their eyes modestly downcast; even more so when they offered thanks and volunteered to hunt for grubs and roots, and to prepare his meals.

'Come with me,' he said, and led them to his wurley.

That evening he enjoyed his meal as never before. When the moon rose he raised himself on his elbow and looked at the women who lay on either side of him. Contentment filled him with an unusual sense of well-being. Feelings he had never experienced, and which he recognised as the first stirrings of love, rose in an overwhelming flood. It was something he had been looking for all his life, but which had been denied to him in his dedication to the task that Nepelle had entrusted to him. 'Ah well,' he thought, 'my work is over. I pray that the All-Father

52

will grant me a time of relaxation and comfort such as I have never known, before he calls me to him.'

Weeks passed in this idyllic manner. There was nothing to be done except a little fishing and hunting, no message for the people who, he was surprised to discover, left him alone with the young women he had rescued. If only the tribespeople had warned him—but none dared give advice to one so powerful as the messenger of Nepelle. During the long nights the little glade where his camp was located rang with laughter. At last he had company, company he had lacked during the years of his mission, and could touch with his hand, warm, living flesh. He even dared to imagine that this was a reward from Nepelle.

As time went by his affection for the girls increased, though there were occasions when he was taken aback by their flightiness. Pondering over this, he came to the conclusion that they needed to be kept occupied.

'You can help me when I'm out hunting as well as in camp,' he told them. 'Take the small hand-net and try to catch the fish that swim close to the bank.'

He waded up to his waist in order to spear the larger fish, while the young women did their best to handle the unaccustomed hand-net.

'See what I've caught,' one of them whispered. 'Three tukkeri!'

'But they're only for the old men. We're not allowed to eat them.'

'Why shouldn't we? The old men will never know. I don't see why men should keep the best food for themselves.'

'All right. We'll put them in our bags and cover them with rushes in case our old man sees them.'

They called to their husband, 'We're going back to the camp. There are no fish here. We'll dig some yams and have them ready for you when you bring your catch home.'

He waved his spear to show he had heard, and went on with his fishing, while his wives ran home to build a fire and bake the fish they had caught.

'No wonder men try to stop us eating these fish,' one of them said, as they sank their teeth into the succulent flesh. 'This is better than wallaby meat or the big, coarse fish that Nurunderi brings back to camp.'

The smell of the cooked food was wafted on the breeze across the water. Old man Nurunderi straightened himself and sniffed suspiciously.

'Tukkeri!' he exclaimed aloud. 'Surely my wives are not cooking the forbidden fish!'

He waded ashore and ran to the camp. A strong smell of cooking and tukkeri oil hung over the encampment, but there was no sign of his wives. They had seen him coming, and had fled to the lakeside by another path. Pulling an old, disused raft from the reeds, they paddled towards the far side of the lake, where they hoped to remain hidden until Nurunderi's anger died down.

It was this episode that caused the messenger of Nepelle to realise that young women could not respond to the love of an old man. It was obvious that they had been using him for their own purposes; and that once he had freed them from imprisonment in the grass-trees, they would remain his property only so long as he protected them from those who knew them to be trouble-makers.

Shading his eyes, he looked across the lake and descried, far out on the water, the black dot that was all that could be seen of the raft bearing the fugitives to the farther shore. Pausing only to gather up his weapons, he ran to his canoe and set off in pursuit.

It was late afternoon when he reached the shore. In the fading light he could make out the faint marks of their feet. Satisfied that he would be able to follow the trail in the morning, he lit a fire, cooked some of the fish he had caught, and examined his weapons. Among them was a plongge, a short club with a knob at the end, used to inflict bruises on those who broke tribal laws. With a grim smile on his face, he fingered it lovingly before lying down with the club cradled in his arms.

The trail was easy to follow in daylight as it led across the soft ground near the edge of the lake, but presently he came to stony ground and lost it. He made several casts, but without success. Feeling dispirited and, he confessed to himself, lonely without the company and lively chatter of the two young women, he made a camp fire and prepared himself for another night of solitude. While he was half asleep, Puckowie, the Grandmother Spirit, came to him and warned him that danger threatened. He remained awake and on guard during the night. In the first light of morning he looked round to see whatever it was that was threatening him.

All he could see was a harmless wombat. In spite of the powers with which he had been invested by Nepelle, he failed to recognise in it the Evil One who had taken this shape to deceive him.

Nurunderi was hungry. He stalked the wombat and killed it. When he withdrew his spear from its body, blood poured on the ground. He carried the animal back to the fire, which had burnt down to a few embers, adding leaves and twigs to coax it back to life, preparatory to cooking the meat in the ashes. As he did so he remembered he had left his spear behind. He went back to retrieve it, and saw a strange sight. The wombat's blood had congealed and was stirring in the sand. Nurunderi watched it gather itself together, increasing in size, and taking the form of a man lying prone on the ground. The face was fully formed, while its limbs and body were in the posture of a sleeping man.

Nurunderi sat lost in thought, endeavouring to read its mind. Eventually he came to the conclusion that no harm could come from it.

'Perhaps he has been given to me by Father Nepelle to help in my search for those wicked women,' he thought; but some instinct prompted him to go into the bush to procure another spear. His own spear, he had noticed, was firmly clutched in the hand of the sleeping man.

When he returned, both the man and the spear had disappeared. Nurunderi could see the shallow depression where the body had been lying, but no footprints to indicate where he had gone.

'Friends always leave footprints,' his thoughts ran. 'It is only an enemy who destroys his trail.'

It was an uncomfortable thought; and at the back of his mind was the even more disturbing suspicion that there was no way by which a human being could wipe out the tell-tale signs of footprints in the sand. Even if the man of blood had swept the trail with the leafy branch of a tree, he would have seen signs of his presence. The recollection of Puckowie's warning came back with redoubled force.

Standing there, he heard a sound which seemed to come from behind a sandhill. Cautiously sidling round it, he came face to face with the Evil One, who had taken human form.

'Are you the man who came from the blood of the wombat?' Nurunderi asked.

'I may be, and again I may not.'

Nurunderi regarded him carefully.

'Yes, you are,' he said. 'You're that man. I can tell, for that is my spear you are holding.'

'Then you may have it,' said the Evil One, and swung it back ready to hurl it at Nurunderi.

'Wait!' cried the messenger. 'I let you have that spear in case you needed it. It was an act of friendship, and because I need your help.'

'What help?' the Evil One said, with the spear still poised.

'I'm looking for my wives. They deceived me and then ran away. I want to find them.'

'Why?'

'To punish them as they deserve.'

'Then you will get no help from me, Nurunderi. I know who you are. You are the messenger of Nepelle, the Teacher he sent out into the world to lead men into the ways of the gods. By foolishly taking these women to yourself you have offended against his laws. I, who am the Evil One, have been sent to punish you.'

Nurunderi's heart sank. He did not believe what the Evil One had said, but he knew that he had done wrong in yielding to the two irresponsible young women, and that his influence had been undermined by his foolishness. It was indeed possible that Nepelle had sent the Evil One to punish him.

'This, too, is a weakness,' Nurunderi reasoned with himself. 'I am being tested. Nepelle may punish me, even reject me, but he would never enlist the services of the Evil One.'

'You can't be the Evil One,' he said firmly. 'Nepelle would never have sent you; nor would the Evil One enter the body of a wombat.'

'I can take any form I wish,' the Evil One boasted. 'In this case I admit I was imprisoned in the wombat. I tried to kill you many times, but the good spirits thwarted me and eventually shut me in the body of the wombat. It was your own fault that I was released, Nurunderi. You forgot the teaching of Nepelle when you fell under the spell of those two foolish girls. When you killed the wombat, it was you who released me.'

'If that is so, you should regard me as your friend.'

'No, you are not my friend, and you have forfeited the protection of Nepelle. You are now just a lonely old man who is about to die!'

Without further warning the Evil One hurled his spear at Nurunderi, who leaped aside. By so doing he saved his life, but the spear pierced his leg. He stopped and drew it out.

'Now you are at my mercy,' he cried, and threw it back with all the strength of his arm, straight into the heart of the Evil One.

Offering a prayer of gratitude to Nepelle, the old man resumed his journey, though he was not sure of the direction he should take. He walked for many hours, until he realised he was making no progress. He recognised the same sandhills, the same trees and, when he turned, the same body of the Evil One lying on the ground. He crouched down and looked at it closely. Birds and insects that approached it, or ran over it, were unable to escape but seemed, in some miraculous fashion, to be drawn into its body.

He realised that it was useless trying to kill its body. Until it was completely destroyed it would continue to be a menace, not only to him, but to every living thing. Perhaps this was a task that Nepelle had set his unfaithful messenger.

He gathered scrub and dry sticks and built a funeral pyre. When it was well alight he dragged the body on to it and waited until it was completely consumed. When he was on the point of leaving he noticed that once again the blood had soaked into the ground. He raked the embers across it. The blood dried and blackened in the heat, and a myriad insects and birds were released, filling the air with their shrill chirping and song.

At last he felt free, as though a burden had been lifted from his body.

Many kilometres and many hours later he came to the bank of the Murray River. Two sets of footprints showed that the runaway wives had come this way. The tracks stopped at the water's edge, indicating that they had found some means of crossing the river. Calling to Nepelle with renewed faith, the messenger was relieved to find that his prayer was answered. The earth trembled, heaped itself like a wave of the sea and formed a tongue of sand and rock that reached across the river,

57

forming a bridge which he crossed at a run. Looking back, he saw that it had disappeared, and knew that his spirit and that of Nepelle were at one.

Some time later he reached the sea. The ashes of a camp fire lay on the sand. Shells and the remains of a meal showed that the young women were still eating forbidden food. Nurunderi sat down and wept. His tears ran together, soaking into the ground, forming a pool that overflowed and trickled into the sea. The pool is still there, but is no longer salt. It is clear and fresh, and sustains the spirits of the departed when they seek the land of eternal life.

The following morning, as soon as it was light, Nurunderi saw a peninsula at a little distance from the shore. The isthmus that connected it with the mainland was guarded by Garagah, the Blue Crane, and there, at last, the messenger saw his wives, talking to the guardian. Far away though they were, Nurunderi saw they were using their artful devices to induce Blue Crane to let them pass to the higher ground at the end of the peninsula.

Nurunderi shouted, telling them to come back. They took no notice. To his disgust one of them put her arms round Garagah's neck and then, as Blue Crane stepped back, both women ran along the isthmus towards the peak of the peninsula.

Puckowie's voice came to Nurunderi as he looked on helplessly.

'This is your opportunity,' the Grandmother Spirit said.

'Help me, Nepelle,' cried Nurunderi. 'In your wisdom you know what I should do to the women I loved so well and so foolishly. They are young. Remember this and forgive my wrong-doing, that has been so much greater than theirs.'

'They're entering the spirit land,' Puckowie whispered urgently. 'Nepelle wishes you to chant the song of the winds. Quickly!'

Nurunderi sang. A puff of wind caught the words and blew them towards the peninsula. The waves leaped to hear them. The wind caught their crests and blew them to a fine spray that drenched the racing girls. The sea lifted itself from its bed and surged across the isthmus, sweeping the young women into its embrace. The waves broke over their heads and they were lost to sight.

The wind soon died away. The isthmus had sunk beneath the waves. The sun shone on a calm sea and on the little island that had become the Island of the Spirit Land. Beyond it two rounded rocks rose above the water.

'They are your wives,' Puckowie said. 'Nepelle has turned them to stone. They will never be permitted to enter the Spirit Land.'

'They do not deserve that,' he said brokenly. He threw himself into the water. His body was seized in the grip of a current that swept him down to the bed of the sea, where he met the spirits of his young wives. As they clung together, they were lifted up into the clear air, through thick folds of clouds, until they reached the heavens, where Nepelle set them as stars to show he had forgiven them.

It was due solely to Nurunderi's great love that forgiveness came—but the petrified bodies of the two young women remain as islets in the ocean as a warning to women never to eat forbidden food.*

---

* The islands are those now known as The Pages, in the Backstairs Passage
  between Kangaroo Island and the mainland, while the peninsula is the body
  of Nurunderi.

PART TWO

TOTEMIC ANCESTORS

THERE are two stages or orders of creation—the activities of the Great Father Spirit who is eternal, omnipresent, and omnipotent; and the totemic ancestors who are equally eternal, recreating themselves in spirit form in the bodies of animals and human beings who retain the mystical animal qualities inherent in the ancestors. Any attempt to reduce Aboriginal concepts to the more prosaic thought-forms of people of European descent is almost sure to fail. The deeper elements of culture can seldom be transferred from one ethnic group to another without distortion. This is particularly true of totemism, which must be felt and experienced as part of one's life, rather than documented and analysed.

What can be transmitted, however imperfect they may be, are the myths of the Ancient Ones. It is these that provide insight into the religion and life of a people who, because of these beliefs, have survived for thousands of years in an apparently hostile environment that has been transformed through acceptance and absorption into the Dreamtime and Dream World of the ageless and protective ancestors.

The three main sections of the present book deal with aspects of that wonderful era known as the Dreamtime. The first part concentrates on the activities of the Great Spirit, who was known mainly to the tribes of south-east Australia. As we might expect, he was responsible for some of the more imposing works of creation. The present section is another or an alternative aspect of the formative era of the Dreamtime. It will be apparent to the reader that the activities of both the Great Spirit and the totemic ancestors were also concerned with the origins of living beings and the landscape of which they were a part.

It is important to remember that although the Dreamtime was that period in which the ancestral heroes, the Old People lived, it was the time of the birth of the world when man, animal and spirit worked in harmony. It was not time forgotten or half-remembered. It is the recurring mystery that men have always experienced, summed up in the feeling of déjà vu. To the Aboriginal, however, it was not a mystery. It was simply the Dreamtime, the sacred objects of which were symbols of the ever-living presence that explained his totemic affiliation which he entered into whenever he took part in increase and initiation ceremonies. The manhood rites were symbolic of death and entrance into this dream world, just as death itself ushered him into rebirth of the Dreamtime.

'When the myths about the drama of the Dream Time are studied with care,' wrote Dr W. E. H. Stanner in *Aboriginal Man in Australia*,* 'it becomes clear that the Aborigines had taken, indeed, had gone far beyond, the longest and most difficult step toward the formation of a truly religious outlook. They had found in the world about them what they took to be signs of intent toward men, and they had transformed those signs in *assurances* of life under mystical nurture.'

The creation myths that follow should therefore be viewed as far more than examples of primitive man's attempts to explain the origins of natural phenomena. Rather they should be read as evidence of advanced thinking, albeit still of a primitive culture, about the purpose and meaning of life and the harmony that underlies the foundation of the universe.

Of the ancestors themselves some were in animal and some in human form. 'They travelled about the country,' wrote Ronald B. Dixon in Volume IX of *The Mythology of All Races*,† 'usually leaving offspring here and there by unions with women of the people (of whose origin nothing is said) whom they either met or made; and ultimately journeyed away beyond the confines of the territory known to the particular tribe, or went down into the ground again, or became transformed into a rock, tree, or some other natural feature of the landscape. These spots then became centres from which spirit individuals, representing these ancestors, issued to be reincarnated in human beings.'

* Angus and Robertson Ltd.
† Marshall Jones Co.

Formation of Landscapes

No matter how varied may be the theories that have been devised to account for physical features, it was a universal belief that before the ancestors or the Great Spirit sculpted the earth, it lay featureless and void beneath an empty sky. As Professor T. G. H. Strehlow has pointed out in *Aranda Traditions,** there is an essential disunity amongst all Central Australian tribes. That is, a disunity not only between one tribe and another, which is to be anticipated, but between the smaller groups and sub-groups of the same tribe, a disunity that extends to customs, ceremonies, and religious ideas. He writes: 'There is no common system of religion which is embraced by the [Aranda] tribe as a whole; all legends—and hence all ceremonies, since the latter are always dramatizations of portions of the legends—are tied down to definite local centres in each group.'

It will serve our present purpose, however, to take a single Northern Aranda example as typical of an infinite variety of myths relating to the formation of the features of the landscape. Although myths may differ in content, they have much in common. In considering this particular myth, however, the importance of the tnatantja pole, which was the great symbol of masculine fertility, should be noted. As Strehlow says, in this area the tnatantja was the greatest single instrument in shaping the northern landscape into its present contours, the blows of the pole having left their marks in valleys and chasms and gorges in every portion of the MacDonnell Ranges and elsewhere.

The Tnatantja Pole

A CERTAIN tnatantja, held in the greatest esteem, might be spoken of as the father of all tnatantjas. It existed long before men and women were created. It was so tall that it touched the sky, a striking object decorated with bands of down that were

* Melbourne University Press.

constantly dispersed by the wind and eventually became living men. In a later age men slept at its foot until they were invited to accompany another group on a war expedition to neighbouring territory. The guardians of the tnatantja then decorated the pole with red down, and placed it under the protection of their aunt, who was a Termite woman. Under such protection it is not surprising that in a high wind the pole snapped at the base. The life force it possessed enabled it to erect itself again of its own volition. The wind came from another direction and laid it low a second time, and again from other directions, each time with the same result. Wherever it fell it caused tremors that caused ridges and troughs to appear in the ground.

When the south wind blew, the red down on the pole was scattered abroad and was seen by another ancestor, who tried to find where it was coming from. While doing so he looked up and was just in time to leap aside before the tnatantja crashed down again, missing him by a hair's breadth. It would appear that this was a deliberate act of the tnatantja, for it rose at once to its former position. The ancestor rushed up to it and seized it at the base, attempting to uproot it. Failing to move it, he shook it so violently that it snapped in the middle.

Holding the broken portion between his toes, the ancestor dragged it away, doubtless forming another deep groove in the ground. Still imbued with life, the fragment grew longer until it was too heavy to be moved. The ancestor then broke it into two halves, one of which he planted in the ground, where it grew and turned into a sacred bloodwood tree.

Two further tales from the same region will serve to indicate how in their journeys ancestors formed the landscape and, in some instances, were created by the accident of environment.

A Crayfish ancestor was surprised by an unexpected torrent of water that inundated the plain where he was walking. As it spread he walked beside it until it came to a gap in the hills. Seeing that the water raced through the narrow gap, he hastily cut a heap of grass and used it to stem the current. The artificial lake thus created grew deeper, providing a habitat for a large number of fish.

Taking a spear with several barbless prongs, the Crayfish ancestor took up a position on the bank and caught a number of fish, throwing them farther up the bank. When he had secured a sufficient number, he lit a fire and roasted them. As soon as they were ready to eat, he placed them on platters of gum leaves, and treated himself to an unusual meal.

Meanwhile the flood water banked up, increasing the pressure in the makeshift stopbank. A section collapsed, leaving a gap through which the water rushed. The ancestor frantically threw more grass into the stream, but his efforts were unsuccessful. There was nothing for it but for the ancestor to follow the water along its course, which formed a deep channel southward, and became part of the 'journey' of the Crayfish ancestor.

The second illustration comes from the Central MacDonnell Range where the mountain known as Iloata had not yet emerged from the womb of the world. Far below the surface it was being shaped and hardened in blood. In the course of time it rose into the light of day, first the peak and then, slowly and majestically, the huge bulk that dominated the land.

At first it was smooth, unlined by rivulets, without any excrescence of bush, grass, boulder, or tree. Deep within there were stirrings of something that eventually came to the surface of the peak in the form of hummocks. They have been described as termite hills; and indeed the description is apt, for from these mounds came the Termite women. As the mounds developed, there developed also an affinity between them and the mountain that gave them birth. At times they were overwhelmed with passion. Then the mountain was shaken to its foundations. In the words of the myth:

> The deep-fissured, steep-faced peak is quivering
>   in every fibre;
> The deep-fissured, steep-faced peak is shaken
>   to its very depths.

These fragments of much longer myths already related provide a prelude to other ancestral 'journeys', most of which are considerably longer and more detailed in their original versions. One aspect, however, must be kept in mind. Each group or sub-group possesses part of rather than the whole 'journey' which, if it were possible to collect it, would cover hundreds of kilometres and would represent the sum of many individual group legends.

The legend of Karora is yet another of the myths narrated to Professor Strehlow by members of the Aranda tribe.

Karora the Bandicoot Ancestor

On the Burt Plain there is a famous soak called Ilbalintja, which was once the home of the Bandicoot ancestor Karora.

Before time had a beginning, when the whole world was in darkness, Karora lay at the bottom of the deep hole that would some day be filled with water. The plain was covered with flowers, but no living being was there to see them in the darkness, nor any animals to browse on the grass.

Above the dry waterhole there towered a gigantic tnatantja that reached up to the unseen clouds. It was no ordinary pole or tree. It was alive, with skin like a man's. It had grown out of the head of Karora, sharing the thoughts that had circled round the bandicoot ancestor's head since the beginning of time. Now, after endless aeons of darkness and quiet, the time had come for the beginning of life. From the belly and the armpits of the ancestor there tumbled an endless stream of bandicoots. They scrambled out of the hole and ran here and there across the plain in search of water, food, and light.

And the light appeared, first as a pale suffusion of the eastern sky. The pole that grew out of Karora's head was bathed in light, bright and golden in the first flush of dawn. The sunlight crept quickly down the pole until the red flowers that carpeted the plain glowed like flame. With the light came heat, penetrating deep into the hole where Karora was lying. He woke from his long sleep, turning his head restlessly from side to side, breaking the roots of the living pole that had grown from his head. He opened his eyes, slowly at first, until they adjusted to the unaccustomed flood of light.

He stood up, climbed out of the hole, and for a while watched the gambolling bandicoots who were his own children. He was aware of hunger and knew instinctively how to satisfy the pangs that gnawed at his stomach. The bandicoots had clustered thickly round him. Seizing two of them he carried them to a spot where the sand had become white-hot in the burning rays of the sun, and cooked and ate them.

All day long Karora watched the bandicoots at play, scurrying about in their search for insects. The sun climbed the arch of the sky and began its descent to the west. As it sank from sight Karora descended to the shelter of the hole and fell asleep. Darkness settled once more over the silent plain—but now mysterious life forces were at work. A long pointed form took shape in the armpit of the sleeping ancestor. A bullroarer emerged from his armpit, long and slender. Its outline blurred, twisted and turned, changing shape, writhing, dividing, forming protuberances that gradually took the form of a full-grown man. This was a true son of Karora, for he had taken the image of his father, the first mortal man to be born at Ilbalintja; motherless, owing life to the creative energy of the father of all bandicoots.

When the sun rose once more, Karora looked with surprise at the living image of himself, lying motionless at his side. As he watched, the young man's eyes opened and he sat up stiffly, placing his hands on his father's breast. The blood coursed through his veins. They were of one flesh, father and son, animated by the spirit that had sustained Karora through the countless seasons that awaited this moment.

'You are my son,' Karora said simply. 'The time has come for us to share a meal. The bandicoots have woken and are at play. Climb up to the plain and kill two of them and cook them where the sun has heated the sand. Then we two shall eat together.'

His son obeyed. They ate the flesh of the bandicoots and were satisfied. That night two more sons were born to Karora. The following night four more appeared. And so it happened night after night until there were as many men at Ilbalintja as bandicoots. The bandicoots grew fewer in number as they were killed for food by the growing family of Karora. As they proved more difficult to catch, the hunters were forced to roam far afield on the plains. One day there were no more bandicoots to be caught and killed.

'You must go farther afield,' Karora told his many sons. 'To the east and to the west, to the north and the south, to Ininta and Ekallakuna. You have taken all who came from my body, my sons.'

The Bandicoot sons spread out in every direction, scouring the plains in search of animals, fossicking amongst the mulga trees, but without success. Tired and hungry, the Bandicoot men were making their way back to Ilbalintja when they heard the sound of a bullroarer somewhere in the distance.

'Another man!' they exclaimed, and rushed towards the sound. No one was there. As they came close to the place where the sound seemed to come from, an animal rushed out of the bushes.

At first sight they thought it must be a large bandicoot. It was only later that they knew it was another creature, which they called a wallaby. But at that moment it was important to kill it. They threw spears at it. Its leg was broken but it was still able to hop faster than the men could run. As it disappeared in the darkness they heard it singing mournfully:

> 'You have lamed me with a spear.
> The night is dark, my heart is filled with fear.
> You could not know that I'm a man
> As you were men when the world began.'

The Bandicoot sons returned to their father, and slept with empty bellies in the deep hole where they were born. But not for long. Out of the east came a great flood of honey from the honeysuckle. It swept them out of the soak and to a mulga thicket some distance away. There they lived with the Wallaby man whose broken leg soon healed. He became their leader, and is regarded by many as their totemic ancestor. The stones that surround the soak at Ilbalintja are pointed out as the petrified bodies of these men.

Karora, larger and heavier than his sons, remained in the waterhole. He sleeps peacefully below the water, but at any time he could rouse himself and rise to the surface, therefore his spirit must be appeased by gifts of branches and leaves by all who come to the soak to draw water.

The Bandicoot sons had been away for three days, searching everywhere for food. On the second day Karora heard the whirring of bullroarers in the distance. He came out of the pit, hoping it was a sign that his sons were returning from the hunt. As they came closer he detected a sound he had not heard before. They were not the bullroarers that belonged to his sons. They had been made by other hands, and they sang a different song. They came from another ancestor and belonged to another tribe, the sons of Ultangkara.

Karora was determined not to let them invade his territory. He could see them advancing towards the waterhole at Ilbalintja and rushed towards them.

'Who are you? What are you doing here?' he shouted as he drew near the crowd of men.

'I am Ultangkara,' their leader said proudly. 'Who are you?'

'I am Karora.'

'Where do you live? Is this your land?' asked Ultangkara.

Karora feared that the newcomers would take advantage of him while his own sons were far away, and tried to head them off.

'I am from Mallal Intinaka,' he said. 'That is my land. You are welcome to rest there. This is no place for you. As you can see, there are no animals here, no food, no place for your sons and mine to live. Go on your way. Go to Mallal Intinaka. I shall follow.'

'Why not come with us and show us the way?' Ultangkara asked suspiciously.

'There is a thorn in my foot,' Karora replied. 'At Malla Intinaka you will find food and water. I shall meet you there.'

Satisfied with the explanation, Ultangkara went with his men in the direction that Karora had indicated and was soon lost to sight.

Karora chuckled to himself. He returned to the hole he had protected from invasion and decorated himself with many designs in clay, awaiting the return of his sons.*

---

* Professor Strehlow has commented: 'This action of deliberate treachery on the part of Karora is extolled as something praiseworthy by the Ilbalintja men. Karora, they say, showed his superior power to the dreaded tjilpa men and protected the sacred soak against roving strangers. Had the myth been recorded from narrators belonging to the *tjilpa* totem, however, the low deceitfulness of the gurra (bandicoot) ancestor would have been condemned in the most scathing and uncompromising terms.'

Three Brothers

UNLIKE the majority of ancestors, who were products of the land they occupied, Yahberri, Mahmoon, and Birrum came from a distant land. The three brothers, together with their grandmother, arrived in a canoe made from the bark of the hoop pine tree, goondool.

They found rivers and coastal waters teeming with fish, flocks of birds flying overhead, and animals browsing among trees, grass, and herbs. There were few people in the newly-found land at that time.

Landing at the mouth of a river, they set up camp and lived with their grandmother for some years. Eventually the brothers felt an urge to visit other parts of this favoured land. Leaving their grandmother behind, they set out in the canoe they had preserved, heading up the east coast until they sighted a cluster of black rocks on the shore. They had exhausted their supply of water, and hoped they might find some in basins and hollows in the rocks. They landed, but in spite of searching diligently, could find no water. One of the brothers drove his spear into the sand at the foot of the rocks, and a spring of clear, cold water welled up.

Quenching their thirst and filling all the vessels in the canoe with fresh water, they continued on their way, and arrived at a tall headland. They disembarked and, leaving the canoe there, separated and went inland. Each of the brothers visited a different part of the continent for the purpose of populating the land. How they accomplished this notable feat is not known, but it may well be that they did so by the exercise of supernatural powers, either by impregnating the few women they found, or by the institution of fertility rites. The second possibility is the more likely. For in due course they made bora rings for the exercising of initiation ceremonies, as well as providing tribal laws.

The blue haze that comes to distant mountains, especially in the spring, is a living reminder of their sojourn. Swathed in a blue mist, the daughters of Yahberri, Mahmoon, and Birrum revisit the earth every year, to promote new life and growth.

That, in brief, is the saga of the three brothers who came from the sea that there might be people on the earth.

The Ancestor with Six Sons

TOTEMIC ancestors were active in peopling the earth as well as adapting the land for their benefit. A myth related by Albert Namatjira and recorded by Roland Robinson concerns an unnamed ancestor who concentrated on the former task.

He was equipped with a large number of the usual hunting weapons, a tjurunga, a sacred stone, a symbolic representation of supernatural life, strength, and fertility, together with six miniature replicas, termed namatoonas, which he kept in his dilly-bag.

Whenever he needed food, he took the namatoonas from the bag, and anointed them with goanna fat. When this was done they took the form of men, as six skilful hunters who were his sons.

The first time he performed this feat he instructed them in the use of spear and woomera and sent them out to hunt for the animals that abounded in that part of the country.

While they were away their father lit a fire, piling on green leaves and grass, and sending a billowing column of smoke high in the air. He knew that it would attract attention and, sure enough, before long six women came from various directions to see who had lit such a large fire and what he wanted in this part of the country.

'Come and sit here with me,' he said, patting the ground. 'I have much to tell you.'

The women came forward hesitantly and sat beside him.

'What are you doing here?' one of the women asked. 'You are old. You have no food. What are you going to eat?'

He laughed and said, 'No need to worry about that.'

His hand swept in a circle as though embracing them all. 'Stay here with me. There will be plenty to eat when night falls.'

They looked at him with disbelief, but something in his face, or maybe an aura that emanated from him, stilled their protests.

Quickly the afternoon hours passed as he told them strange tales of other regions, of mysteries and wonders of land and sky in words that echoed in their brains, drawing them to him and in turn repelling them, until they were barely conscious of their surroundings or the passing of time.

They were clutched by the first chill fingers of night. They woke from their trance as the old man, the wirinun as they thought him to be, threw dry sticks on the fire. It blazed up fiercely as six tall young men, laden with meat, strode into the circle of firelight and threw down their burdens.

'These are your husbands,' the mysterious stranger said. 'First we will cook the meat and eat it to celebrate the marriage that will be consummated this night. These are my sons. A noble man, each one. They will choose their brides from among you. Before the sun rises you will achieve the destiny for which you have waited, unwittingly, until now.'

The food was cooked and eaten. There had been dances and song and the sleep of fulfilment and exhaustion. The stars that had shone with steady light on the encampment were paling in the light of dawn. Quietly the old man went from one sleeping couple to another, stooping, taking the namatoonas from the hair of the young men. When the last stone had been placed in the dilly-bag, the ancestor gathered the spears and woomera and strode off into the light of morning.

The six women woke and looked at each other in bewilderment. The old man had gone and of their husbands of a night there was no sign except the faint impression in the sand where they had lain in their arms. A trail of footprints led from the encampment, dwindling and vanishing in the distance—a single track, as though one man had left, not the trail of seven men. Only the dead ashes of the fire and a heap of charred bones remained to show that it was not a dream.

At noon, in a place in the distant valley, the ancestor again rubbed the namatoonas, again his sons went hunting, again the smoke rose from the fire, again curiosity brought six women to his encampment, and again, that night, the six women were given to the men who had emerged from the sacred stones.

And so, day after day, and night after night, the same procedure was followed resulting, many moons later, in the birth of babies who would some day populate the land. Until one fateful morning, when one of the women woke early and saw, with startled eyes, the ancestor withdrawing a namatoona from the hair of one of his sons, and the subsequent disappearance of the young man. As she opened her mouth to scream, the ancestor whirled round and transfixed her to the ground with his spear.

He sighed with relief. The journey had been long and he was old and weary. Hundreds of babies were waiting to be born from end to end of his journeying. The last namatoona was gathered and placed in his dilly-bag. Leaving five sleeping and one dead woman behind, the ancestor trudged away on the last stage of his long journey.

Turning his face to the east, he placed the dilly-bag by his side and lay down to rest. When morning came the sun shone on his face. He smiled in his sleep as he felt the warmth, and breathed his last breath before being turned to stone.

Knowing that their father was dead, the namatoonas struggled to escape from the dilly-bag. It burst open, scattering its contents in a circle round the petrified ancestor, and in turn the tjurunga, the spears and woomeras, and the namatoonas who were his offspring, were all turned to stone.

The Rainbow Snake

IN Northern Australia the cult of the Rainbow Snake is widespread. Although differing from the concept of totemic beings in other parts of the continent, the Serpent was certainly an 'ancestor'. The term pulwaiya, which is derived from a word meaning 'father's father', provides a clue to its place in the supernatural world. Being closely associated with water, which is essential to life, it is symbolic of fertility and an important element in fertility rites.

The cult is not confined to the northern regions. It was also established in New South Wales. As Roland Robinson has said in *Aboriginal Myths and Legends*,* 'Its sacred significance is that of both the phallus and the womb. It is the great father, and

---

* Sun Books.

mother, of all forms of life. It is always associated with water, the source of life.'

In *An Illustrated Encyclopedia of Aboriginal Life* by A. W. Reed, the following account provides a brief summary of its characteristics and functions.

Belief in the Rainbow Serpent, which goes under many different names, was spread over a wide area. There are myths which show the snake's attraction to blood, and others in which it is the spirit of water, rain, and flood. At certain periods women were required to keep close to a fire, and this applied to mothers immediately after childbirth. As the essential spirit of water, the Rainbow Serpent would not go near the fire. An important function of this great spirit creature was to excavate the beds of rivers as he travelled about.

The extent to which the Rainbow Serpent entered into fertility rites is indicated by the frequency of his appearance in sacred designs and drawings. Water was the life-giving element; similarly the serpent which brought rain was the life-giving force in religious rites. This vast serpent reached down from the sky to the waterholes and pools, bringing water to the earth. Medicine men whom he killed and brought to life again were able to conjure up the rain clouds by appealing to him when performing the necessary rites.

Elkin observes that the Rainbow Serpent was associated with the Arnhem Land concept of the Fertility Mother, and the Wondjina rain ritual of the northern Kimberleys. It did not exist as a separate cult. The snake was sometimes regarded as male and sometimes as female. Kunapipi, the aged woman who made a long journey across country in the Dreamtime, was preceded by the Rainbow Serpent, who cleared the way for her by uprooting trees and causing rivers to flow towards the sea. In this myth the serpent symbolised the floods and storms that caused the rivers to rise. By the name of Wonambi it lived in pools and lagoons and had an important function in the training of medicine men, while in Arnhem Land it protected sacred lore by sending floods to drown people who offended against it. In this area, so rich in art forms, it was called Julunggul or Yurlunggul. In the Kimberleys it was associated with the birth of spirit children.

Everywhere it was symbolic of rain water, the products of rain, and the fertility of growing things. In Arnhem Land where the Fertility Mother cult was observed, it occupied an important place in the annual rites that took place before the wet season. A whistling sound was heard preceding its coming. It was the noise of the storm whistling through its horns. As the dances and songs began, the Rainbow Serpent was seen to arch its body upwards to the sky.

In the beliefs of many Aboriginal tribes, the rains would dry up, the earth would become parched, and life would cease to exist if it were not for the Rainbow Serpent.

In referring to the pulwaiya who chose for their final resting place some locality which they impregnated with their spirit, powers of reproduction, and endowed with human characteristics, in *Myths of the Munkan** Ursula McConnel writes that some of the myths, 'such as the moon and tides, or Taipan, the rainbow-serpent, to whom are attributed thunder and lightning, floods and cyclonic disturbances, reach an even higher place in the hierarchy of the *pulwaiya* and derive their complex character from a variety of motifs'.

Taipan

THE myth of Taipan, the Brown Snake, exemplifies many of the characteristics already mentioned. In the beginning, as a medicine-man, he possessed supernatural powers. He could give relief to anyone who had inadvertently swallowed a bone by sucking it out of his body. He commanded thunder and lightning by sympathetic magic with a sharpened flint attached to a string. By throwing it against a tree or stone, a sheet of flame flared out and the noise of the concussion would echo

---

* By permission, Melbourne University Press.

through the hills. By means of his pointing bone he could kill, and with equal facility he could cure men and women of their ailments. He had the power to cause rain to fall and floods to devastate the countryside. The fear he engendered in his fellow tribesmen was apparent in the readiness with which they gave their daughters to him. He had three wives, Uka the White Sand-snake, Mantya the Death-adder, and Tuknampa the Water-snake.

His only son, who was also named Taipan, grew to manhood, and embarked on a journey down-river from the swamp where he lived with his parents. Presently he came to a camp site on the bank of the river, where he met Tintauwa, the black Water-snake, who was the wife of Wala, the Blue-tongued Lizard. Tintauwa had been sleeping in the shade of a tree while Wala was hunting. The sound of Taipan's paddle woke her, but she lay still, peeping from under half-closed eyelids, pretending to be asleep.

Taipan tied his canoe to a root and stole silently to the tree where the woman was lying. She opened her eyes and looked up at him as he bent over her. No words were needed to express the love that engulfed them as they looked deep into each other's eyes. Taipan held out his hand. She grasped it to pull herself up. With a sweeping gesture of her free hand she indicated that the world was theirs and that where Taipan went, she too would go. Hand in hand, they left the river, striking inland, running lest Wala should catch up with them. They rested at night and ran on the next day, until they felt there was little chance of being found by the Blue-tongued Lizard man.

Day after day Taipan hunted game while Tintauwa searched for grubs and vegetable food. At night they cooked their meal and slept together with their feet towards the fire. It seemed as though they had the world to themselves. But they had reckoned without the cold rage of Wala, whose wife had been taken from him so suddenly. Unsuspected by the runaway wife and her lover, he was never far behind them. Late one afternoon he could smell smoke as they lit a fire in preparation for the evening meal of emu flesh. As he came closer he saw Taipan's head above the bushes. Hooking his spear to the notch on his woomera, he raised his arm and hurled the weapon at Taipan.

But Wala was neither a hunter nor a warrior. He had never been instructed in the art of selecting suitable wood for his spear, nor in fining and honing, rubbing it with fat and polishing it as a trained fighting man would have done. It has been said that it was made of milkwood and hibiscus. The result was that it snapped in half before it even reached its target.

Taipan and Tintauwa sprang to their feet.

'He's come! He's come!' the woman wailed.

Taipan pushed her down into the shelter of the scrub, saying in a fierce whisper, 'Lie there! Perhaps he won't see you.'

'He knows I'm here,' she whispered back. 'That's why he has come. Your spear is sure to break. You can't fight him.'

Taipan jumped into the open space by the fire, levelled his own frail, wooden-headed spear, and hurled it at Wala. It hit the Lizard man on the forehead raising a lump that has remained on all lizards from that day onwards.

Taipan's spear was broken. Wala hit him with his woomera but that, too, was shattered. Both men were defenceless. They wrestled, but neither could overcome the other. They fell back, panting.

The aggrieved husband was the first to speak.

'In combat you cannot prevail,' he said in short gasps. 'Nor can I. But don't think you can escape my vengeance. I am an honourable man. You've tried to destroy my honour. Now you must pay for it. But I shall not take advantage of you. I'll lie down. You can bite me on my neck. If you kill me you can take my wife. If you fail, then you must lie down and I'll bite your neck.'

Seeing that Wala had given him the first chance, Taipan agreed.

Wala lay down at his feet, rolled over, and put his head back. Taipan fastened his teeth in his throat, twisting and turning, but was unable to tear the thick skin. When he reeled back, exhausted, Wala threw him to the ground, turned him on his back with a contemptuous thrust of his foot, and sank his teeth deep into his jugular vein. Not satisfied with this he tore open his breast and took out the heart and blood of Taipan.

Then, with Tintauwa crying piteously behind him, he made his way upriver to the camp of Taipan the father. Coming into the presence of the great pulwaiya, he threw heart and blood on to a pandanus leaf and said in a loud voice that all could hear, 'There is your son Taipan.'

The older man gazed at it in horror.

'The blood and the heart you may keep, Taipan,' Wala continued. 'The body of your son lies far from here, where scavenger birds are already devouring his flesh.'

Taking the hand of his wife in his, he ran off—and was not heard of again.

The anguished father called his other sons to him—Flying-fox, Swamp-fish, one by one they came to him and on each he smeared the blood of their older brother. The blood remained with them, and flows in the veins of their descendants. They went to their totem sites, where they remained. Their two sisters carried it to their permanent home on the rainbow. The heart of the slain son Taipan he kept for himself.

The rainbow is the totem site of his daughters, where the blood of their brother provides the red course in that shining bow, just as the blue course is that of Taipan, the Rainbow Serpent.

The rain fell from a dark cloud. Taipan threw a blood-red knife into the cloud, which was split by a vivid flash of lightning. Thunder rolled round the hills and, in the dazzling blaze of light that came from the sky, men hid their faces. Taipan sank into the ground, where he lives on, under a milkwood tree that stands close by the lake that was formed on that day of rain and blood. If anyone dares to disturb the blood-red body of the pulwaiya, thunder roars and lightning flashes from the sky.

As for his daughters, they returned to their totem centre under the water where they remain during the dry season. When the rains come they climb up the rainbow once more, bearing aloft their colours to mingle with those of their brother.

Amongst other things, the myth explains how Taipan controls the blood supply. In the words of Ursula McConnel, it gives him 'power over the physiological processes of men and women—the blood-flow, the heart, and menstruation'.

The Rainbow Snake and the Orphan

A MYTH from North Goulburn Island ends with the death of the Rainbow Snake, an unusual fate for an all-powerful spirit being.

At Arunawanbain, a place that means 'Something ate us', there lived a small boy whose mother and father were dead. His maternal grandmother had taken charge of him and looked after him well. But it was not the same as having a father to teach him how to throw a spear or trail small animals. Worst of all, his playmates taunted him because he had no father.

One day he went to his grandmother, crying bitterly.

'What is your trouble, little one?' she asked.

'They wouldn't give me any of their waterlily roots,' he sobbed.

'Who wouldn't?'

'The other boys and girls.'

'Never mind,' she said. 'Those who are greedy now will have empty bellies some day. Here are some grass-seed cakes and honey I've saved for you.'

The child continued to weep and refused to touch the food. All night he kept on crying. His wailing disturbed the Rainbow Snake. It unfolded its coils and slithered round the camp site.

The enormous head completely filled the humpy where the child was crying. Rainbow Snake opened his mouth and swallowed the child and his grandmother. With the remains of the humpy draped over his head, he swayed backwards and forwards, picking up the panicking tribespeople as they ran aimlessly from one refuge to another.

Soon the camp was deserted. Rainbow Snake dragged his huge length slowly and painfully across the island, his belly weighted down by the people he had swallowed. He crossed the strait to the mainland. He had not gone far when he came across another camp site. His hunger not yet satisfied, he engulfed several men and women in his gaping jaws and swallowed them whole.

This time, however, he met with resistance. The men battered his head with their nulla-nullas. His body was infested with a hundred spears which protruded like thorns from his huge bulk. Moving with difficulty, his energy sapped by the weight of his distended belly, he collapsed on the ground and expired. The warriors cut the body open and released the imprisoned tribesmen and women.

It happened so long ago that the tale has passed through countless generations. The groove the snake made in its overland journey is a reminder to all men that even so powerful and relentless an ancestor as a Rainbow Snake was once put to death at the hands of men.

Julunggul

THE Wawalag sisters, who are now stars, were travelling northwards somewhere in the vicinity of the Roper River. Many tales are told of their adventures on this journey, which came to an end at a sacred waterhole. Here the elder sister gave birth to a baby. Her blood attracted the attention of Julunggul, the gigantic python who lived there.

The sisters prepared to remain by the waterhole that night. They built a shelter, brought out the provisions they had gathered, and kindled a fire to cook the animals their dogs had caught earlier in the day.

While they were preparing the meal, everything they had brought with them, together with snails, roots and other objects in the vicinity, were drawn by some mysterious force into the waterhole.

Then the rain came down, not as it usually does, but in a torrential flood that filled the waterhole and inundated the land. Through the veil of water the younger sister caught a glimpse of a gigantic snake. She realised it was none other than Julunggul, the Rainbow Snake.

The women danced round the waterhole to protect themselves against the python. Towards morning they crawled into the shelter and fell into an exhausted sleep.

The all-seeing eyes of Julunggul detected them lying there. His great body looped into a circle that embraced the waterhole and the flimsy shelter, in order to prevent the women escaping.

He opened his mouth and swallowed everything that lay within his coils—the baby, the two sisters, and the shelter disappeared into the vast maw.

He lay down to sleep, but was bitten by an ant and stung to wakefulness. He disgorged the contents of his stomach, but the women were no longer alive. The two sisters were swallowed a second time and devoured at his leisure.

In relating and comparing several of the Rainbow Serpent myths, R. M. and C. H. Berndt* comment on the amount of symbolism contained in them. 'For example, the python, usually called Julunggul in this setting, is a phallic symbol … the python is … the male principle in nature. This is linked with the fluctuation of the seasons, such as the monsoonal rains and floods, and with the increase of human beings and other creatures, and of plants. As in other myths of this area, there is an emphasis on the significance of blood, which has a sacred quality.'

The Pursuit of Purra

AMONG the myths of the Wotjobaluk tribe, living on or near the Avoca, Richardson, and Wimmera rivers in Victoria, is a long and somewhat involved account of the journeys of a number of ancestors. There is little 'plot' in the European sense, but a considerable degree of characterisation and much information about the events that occurred in the Dreamtime and their effect on the habitat of their descendants.

The myth was recorded by Aldo Massola in *Bunjil's Cave*, and throws light on the proper form of local Aboriginal place names and their meaning, as well as the events that were supposed to have occurred there.

Wembulin, the Triantelope Spider, was a bloodthirsty fellow, always on the lookout for unwary animals to supplement the food he preserved for himself and his two daughters. With his instinct for detecting animals at a distance,

---

* *The World of the First Australians* (Angus and Robertson and Ure Smith).

81

he became aware that Doan the Flying Squirrel was pursuing Purra the Kangaroo. Purra covered the ground swiftly with his long legs, but Doan, with his ability to glide from one tree to another, was gradually overtaking the fugitive.

Purra would have provided a bigger meal, but Wembulin was too far away to reach him. Doan provided an easier prey. Flying Squirrel alighted on a bough close to the home of Spider, ready to glide to the next tree. Wembulin lunged forward, his jaws coming together like a steel trap. He missed the Flying Squirrel by a hair's breadth, his teeth closing on the trunk of a tree, biting through it so that the topmost branches crashed to the ground.

Unaware of what was happening behind him, Purra fled on, across a sandy waste where his track eventually formed the bed of the Wimmera River. By this time he was aware that he had outrun his pursuer. Coming to a place where grass grew in plenty, he browsed for a while, causing a depression which, long afterwards, filled with water and was known to the white men who succeeded the original inhabitants as Lake Hindmarsh.

Where the grass was closely cropped, Purra proceeded in leisurely fashion, forming the channel that drains the lake, until he came to a grove of quandongs which provided him with a change of diet. It was the site of Lake Albacutya. After this he continued his journey in a northerly direction. With the passing of time his tracks became obliterated. His final resting place has never been discovered.

Meanwhile Wembulin was hot on the trail of Doan, pursuing him from one tree top to another. Whenever he drew near, his jaws clashed together, always missing his intended victim, denuding the trees of their topmost branches as the sinister jaws severed the tree trunks where Doan had rested a moment before. The line of pursuit could be seen long afterwards by the row of truncated trees. At last pursuer and pursued reached the end of the bush. Doan floated down from the last, outermost tree, and was immediately at a disadvantage. Wembulin lowered himself on a thread and pounced on his helpless victim.

It was all over in minutes and little remained to show that Doan had been killed and eaten at the forest edge. Wembulin returned to his lair, collected his two daughters, and went to the sandy plain where he believed no one would be able to locate them. It was a wise move, for Doan's relatives had become concerned when he failed to return from his pursuit of Purra. His two uncles on his mother's side of the family, who were both called Bram-bram-bult, set out to see what had happened to him. They were shocked when they met Mara the Sugar-ant and saw he was carrying a hair from their nephew's head in his mouth; and even more perturbed when they came across his relatives, all of whom were carrying hairs, together with pieces of bone and flesh they recognised as parts of Doan's body.

When they reached the edge of the bush and saw the pathetic remains of their nephew lying on the sand, together with the tracks of Wembulin and his daughters, they determined to avenge their nephew's death. Wembulin's trail led northwards. The two uncles found the ashes of his first camp fire, long since dead, at Guru* and again at Ngelbakutya† where Wembulin and his daughters had feasted on quandongs. As the ashes of the fire were still warm, they quickened their pace and caught up with the three Spiders at Wonga.

Feeling themselves quite safe at this remote spot, Wembulin's daughters were busily employed pounding honeysuckle seeds in preparation for the evening meal. The Bram-bram-bult uncles heard the sound long before they came in sight of the camp and prepared to make a surprise attack.

The younger of Doan's uncles circled to windward so that his scent would blow across the encampment while the older one stole stealthily through the brush and took up a position at the side of the shelter Wembulin had built, out of sight of the daughters.

When Triantelope Spider caught the scent of the younger Bram-bram-bult brother, he rushed out of the brushwood shelter, baring his teeth and grinning at the prospect of another meal—only to have his sinister fangs knocked down his throat by the elder brother's waddy. In the time it takes to draw breath, Wembulin lay dead, and in a few more breaths his head was severed from his body and rolled to and fro like a ball.

'Now we'll kill the Spider girls,' the younger brother said, but the older one had different ideas.

---

* Lake Hindmarsh.
† Lake Albacutya.

'They're handsome in their own way. It would be stupid to kill them when we can enjoy them. They can save us a lot of hard work by digging yams and grubs, to say nothing of preparing food.'

Leaving the campsite at Lake Wonga, which had been formed when Wembulin's head had been rolled on the ground, and taking the two girls with them, they went across country until they came to Wirrenge,* where they discovered the tracks of several kangaroos.

'Remain here,' they said to the Spider Women. 'Prepare hot stones in an earth oven, ready for the kangaroos we'll bring back with us.'

Hardly were they out of sight than they heard trees crashing to the ground.

'Spider Women!' they exclaimed together. The thought that the girls might have inherited the tree-biting propensities of their father had never occurred to them. Abandoning the chase, they hurried back to Wirrenge and killed the women before they could do any further mischief. To make sure they were dead they beat them with their waddies; the scattered teeth and bones of the women account for the limestones nodules that are to be found by the lakeside.

At Yarak† they found Jinijinitch, the Great White Owl, and his two sons. As hunting had been poor in that district, they were surprised when Owl offered them meat. Father and sons were evasive in their replies, but by repeated questioning the Spider brothers forced an admission that the flesh was that of Owl's wife. The Bram-bram-bult brothers were horrified to think that anyone would eat the flesh of wife or mother. In their disgust they summoned a storm by the ingenious method of filling their mouths with water and spitting it to the distant horizon where it evaporated, forming storm clouds that drifted over the encampment and inundated the camp in a heavy fall of rain.

Great White Owl took shelter in his humpy and fell asleep, only to be burnt to death when the Bram-bram-bult brothers set fire to the shelter. The charred bones are said to be mixed with

---

* Lake Wirrengreen.
† Lake Coorong.

84

the sandstone at Bori Jinijinitch* where Great Owl had his encampment. The Owls were an unpleasant family. Feeling sorry for the two sons, the brothers spared their lives, but when they found them fighting and biting each other, they dispatched them both and went on their way.

They came to an arid land, where stream beds were dry and animals were dying of thirst. The only one who was thriving was Gertuk the Mopoke who was perched in a tree, looking superciliously at his friends who were suffering torments. He had a pet dog that seemed as contented as his master. Rumour had it that Owl kept a supply of water in the hollow tree he had selected as his home.

The brothers decided to punish the selfish Mopoke. Chanting spells, they caused the fork by his perch to close up, imprisoning him within the hollow tree.

Presently Binbin the Tree-creeper and his relatives came to search for insects in the bark. As they ran up and down the trunk they heard a pitiful voice from inside, begging to be released. Tree-creepers are obliging little birds. They knocked on the trunk, pecking at it with their beaks, trying to find the hollow place where Mopoke was confined. They drilled a hole where they thought he might be, only to raise a shout of protest because they had pecked his head. They attacked the bark a little lower but, misjudging the position of Gertuk, his breast was pierced by the beaks of the Tree-creepers. He was released, his breast streaming with blood which coagulated, leaving a dark stain that his descendants have inherited, and a mass of rubbish that fell on his head.

By the time he had recovered, the brothers were far away, but Gertuk harboured resentment against them. He experimented with a little magic, rolling up all the winds he could find in a kangaroo-skin and letting them out with a rush. When he found that he could generate sufficient pressure to blow over a humpy, and uproot trees, he left his home and followed the trail of the Bram-bram-bults.

He caught up with the brothers at Mukbilly and aimed the mouth of his bag at them. The result was more than he expected. The blast that came out uprooted most of the trees as

---

* The name is commemorative, meaning 'No More Jinijinitch'.

far as the eye can see—which explains the lack of trees in that district. The elder Bram-bram-bult was saved by clinging to one of the few trees that survived the hurricane. His brother, who had chosen a shallow-rooted tree, was blown far away to the swamps at Galk. When he crawled to the water to slake his thirst he was frightened away by the booming Gau-urn the Bittern, and wandered aimlessly along the bank of the Wimmera River.

Elder brother felt responsible for him. He searched for him in vain, and went home to his mother, Dok the Frog.

'Help me find my brother,' he begged.

Dok squeezed her breast, ejecting a quantity of milk which rose in the air in an arc and fell in the direction where the younger Bram-bram-bult was lying, bruised by the tossing he had received in the hurricane and exhausted by his long journey. Mother and son travelled together. Whenever they were at a loss where next to turn, Dok again sent out a jet of milk to enable them to turn in the right direction. When he was sure that he could find the way, Bram-bram-bult sent his mother home and finished the journey on his own. When he reached his brother, he attempted to revive him, but the sadly bruised man had been bitten by a snake. Shortly after the elder brother's arrival, he died.

For a long time elder Bram-bram-bult mourned his brother's death. When he could bear the loneliness no longer, he felled a gum tree and with his stone axe trimmed the trunk and fashioned a wooden figure in the semblance of a man to keep him company. When it was finished, he sang incantations and commanded the figure to come alive. It moved, woodenly at first, but as it gathered confidence, its limbs became supple and it took on the familiar features of his dead brother.

Together they travelled far to the west and made a home for themselves in a cave until they reached their last resting place as the Pointers of the Southern Cross, close to their mother Dok, who is also one of the stars in the Cross.

PART THREE

CREATION MYTHS

MYTHS and legends which explain how birds, mammals, insects, reptiles, and fish came into being must be nearly as numerous as the various tribes that inhabit the land. One of the most appealing tells how a rainbow once shattered into a thousand pieces, each of which became a bird, as varied in colour as the rainbow, and of an infinite number of shapes and sizes.

Other legends tell how birds and animals developed their separate characteristics. The kangaroo, for instance, stood on his hind legs to observe the flood of multi-coloured birds descending from the sky, and adopted the posture permanently. The emu stretched out his neck for the same purpose, and ran away so fast that his legs grew long and sturdy. Others crept into holes in the ground or dug them with their paws and remained there as burrowing animals that emerge only to forage for food.

As for the birds that fell from the sky, there was the kookaburra who broke into peals of laughter at the sight of the myriad specks of colour falling towards the ground. There were others who were so frightened by their sudden descent that they cried out in fear, developing harsh, discordant voices. Most of the birds enjoyed the experience and sang joyously as they tested their wings and discovered that they had been given the freedom of the air.

The nature of the birds varied as much as their forms and colour. Some were happy and light-hearted, spending much of their time on the wing. Some rejoiced in wind and sunshine. The eagle-hawk was one whose powerful wings took him higher and higher, as close to the sun as he could fly. There were others who had limited ability to fly and were content to browse in the undergrowth and satisfy their hunger with a diet of worms and insects. And a few, such as the mopoke, preferred the dark night in which to seek their prey, sleeping by day in order to avoid the sunlight they thought so harsh, and developed large, staring eyes to catch every glimmer of light at night.

In time the multi-coloured family of birds became confirmed in their habits, enjoying each new day, living happily in the world that had been prepared for them.

But not all. A few were dissatisfied with what Baiame had done for them. They longed for another colour in their plumage, a sweeter or louder voice, different beak, legs, or body. Chief among them was Brush Turkey. He felt his body was too clumsy. His wings could not support him in soaring flight. And, more than anything he resented the fact that he was brown all over, from head to tail, from beak to claw. He was jealous of the bright plumage of other birds, of their sweet voices, and the manner in which they could soar far above his head into the blue sky.

Unable to improve his own condition, he determined to destroy his light-hearted relatives. There was only one way he could think of to do this. Far away on the hills there was a burning tree. He could see it gleaming like a spark at night. It had been struck by lightning and, being endued with magical qualities, the fire that blossomed in its branches never died down.

'If I were to take some of this fire and put it in the forest, there'd be a grand conflagration,' he thought. 'It would destroy their nests and in time there'd be no eggs and no fledglings. I'll do it!'

He reflected, 'What about me? What would happen to me?' Then he reflected that his home was in the scrub, and that it would make little difference to him if the forest was destroyed.

He set out on his journey to the burning tree in daylight, arriving there after it was dark. The tree was bigger than he had thought and he was unable to approach too near for the heat that came from it. Poking about in the undergrowth he found a dried stick and thrust it into the tree. It burst into flame. Chuckling to himself Brush Turkey scuttled away from the tree. Flapping his wings, half-walking, half-flying, he came to the forest and set fire to a heap of fallen branches.

The result was more spectacular than he had imagined. Gum trees burst into flame from top to bottom with a sudden roar.

Within seconds the fire ran through the forest, fanned by a gentle breeze, sending up showers of sparks that kindled further fires.

The other birds were sleeping on their perches in the trees, never dreaming of danger. Only Owl was awake. Suddenly he was blinded by light and realised that the forest was on fire. With a whoosh and a scream he rushed from nest to nest shaking the boughs and shouting, 'Wake up! Wake up! The forest's on fire! Hurry, hurry, or you'll be burnt to cinders!'

A great clamour arose as the birds flew from their nests. Those with young tried to carry them on their backs. Eggs had to be abandoned as the nests exploded in flames. A few birds perished, but most escaped, hiding in caves, in long grass well away from the forest, or flying about aimlessly, wondering what to do next.

The bewildered ones fluttered farther and farther away until they reached the sea. By that time they were exhausted by the heat and the long flight. Then a wonderful thing happened. As their wings drooped, they fell headlong into the sea, and down into its cool depths. Their wings shrank, legs disappeared, their bodies elongated, and feathers changed to silvery scales—and in this unusual manner the ocean was populated with fish of as many varieties as the birds that experienced the transformation.

The fire that Brush Turkey had lit was so fierce that every bush and tree was reduced to ashes. It is now the dead heart of the great island continent. But other forests sprang up in the north, the east, and the west. The birds that had survived the conflagration built their nests once more in the new-grown trees and raised families, so that the world was again filled with song and laughter.

The one who suffered most was Brush Turkey. The brown plumage he despised was covered with ash and turned to an even unlovelier grey—all except his head which remained a fiery red from the flames—a badge of shame, a constant reminder to everyone of the terrible deed he had done.

The First Men and Women

THE greatest of all mysteries is surely that of the origin of mankind. It is not surprising that there was much ingenious speculation on this important subject. It is impossible to unravel all the complications of inter-relationship between animals and men. The inter-changeability of animal life forms, including those of mankind, is a recurrent theme in myth and legend. On the other hand there are some in which mankind is regarded as unique, and the subject of a special creation. One such example is to be found in the Aranda myth of the Numbakulla brothers and the Inapatua.

The Inapatua were an embryonic form of life. They were formless, but with shadowy indications of the beings they would ultimately become. They can best be envisaged as boulders with a faint resemblance to the various parts of the human body. Lifeless, they lay on the desert sands.

The Numbakulla were two brothers who observed these strange forms from their home in the sky. They descended to earth and, working patiently with their knives, carved the plastic mass into recognisable shapes, imbued them with life, and sent them to people the continent that awaited their coming.

This myth has the virtue of simplicity. A curious factor is that creation of new life presumes the prior existence of sentient beings; as for instance, in the Munkan myth of Yagaanamaka, whose name may be translated Trample-the-Hair.

A woman who was travelling north and a man on his way south, met on a plain. The following conversation, direct and to the point, took place.

The man asked, 'Where are you from?'

The woman replied, 'From the south. Where do you come from?'

'From the north. Are you by yourself?'

'Yes.'

'Then will you be my wife?'

'I will be your woman.'

The formalities were complete. Man and woman were one. They lit a fire and lay down together. A new regime had begun. For the first time man and woman had been united, but with divided responsibilities, living together, sharing good and ill fortune, each complete and yet part of the other.

The days were spent in fishing, hunting, gathering grubs and vegetables. At the shared evening meal, daytime absence was replaced with union by night. They would have been content to live out their years together in this way were it not for the thought that when they died there was none to remember them.

'We have no baby,' said the woman with sudden insight. 'We two have no baby. All living things have babies, but not we two.'

It was springtime. She had seen eggs and fledglings in nests, the tiny offspring of animals, the diminutive forms of insects, turtles' eggs, even roe in the body of fish they caught.

'If birds, animals, reptiles, and insects can all have babies, then we too should have a baby.'

The man agreed. 'I shall make a baby of clay. You can nurse it.'

'Yes,' she said. 'You can do that, but you must place it in my body to give it life.'

The man was startled at this proposal, but after going away and thinking about it, he had to agree that a baby made of clay would be of no use unless it were alive.

He dug clay, fashioning it skilfully into the form of a little man complete in every detail. It lay inert in his arms.

'Place it in my body where I can cherish it,' the woman said, and this he did, injecting the juice from a milkwood tree to start the flow of milk, and red gum to simulate blood once the clay baby came alive.

And behold, when the woman gave birth to the baby, it emerged flushed with life, moving its limbs and crying. The woman put it to her enlarged breasts and the baby lay contentedly in her arms.

'It lives!' the man exulted. 'It is a little man. Some day he will go hunting with me. This baby is our baby, the first ever to be born of woman.'

He left the mother and baby, bounding over the plain like a kangaroo, hunting not for the one but for the two who now shared his camp fire. When he returned he looked at the baby again.

He said, 'Our baby has no hair!'

He gathered grass and placed it on the baby's head.

'Now you look like a real boy,' he said proudly. 'We shall live here and watch him grow into a man.'

The woman was content.

'What shall we call our baby?' she asked.

'We shall call it Yagaanamaka—Trample-the-Hair, for here I have trampled on the grass that is now the hair of our baby. In all the years to come more babies will be born, more and more, until the world is full of babies. This will be their totem centre where men will trample the grass for the babies their wives will bear.'

One of the most astounding series of metamorphoses began with a mosquito. Instead of completing its life cycle in the usual manner, it increased in size and shape and turned into a blowfly. Some time after assuming this form it swelled up again and became a moth. The most startling transition occurred when the moth changed into a small bird, the process ending when the small bird in turn became a crow.

Once it achieved its final shape the erstwhile mosquito took on the characteristics of that meddlesome, high-spirited fellow usually known as Wahn,* who was the progenitor of the crow family. A more widely circulated legend tells how Wahn accompanied Mulyan, the Eagle-hawk, and how Wahn tricked the larger bird into jumping onto the nest of a kangaroo-rat, where his feet were impaled on a pointed bone. The Wotjobaluk version ascribes the Crow's motive to his need to find a wife.

The animal world was still in process of formation. No one had yet been created who would be suitable for a lively Crow to take to wife. True, there were some half-formed creatures of indeterminate shape who inhabited the trees without ever setting foot on the ground. Crow felt that his only hope was to capture one of them and in some way to adapt it to a woman who would serve as his wife.

---

* The adventures of Wahn the Crow are related in some detail in *Aboriginal Legends*.

It appears that Crow had not yet adopted the likeness of a bird, or else that he had passed through this stage of evolution and had reached the stature of a man.

He made his plan carefully. The tree-top creatures were beyond his reach. It was necessary to lure one of them down or, to use a later term, to smoke one out. This is what he did, in a literal fashion. First he took the bone of a kangaroo, trimmed one end to a sharp point, and pushed it into the ground, point uppermost. Next he gathered a quantity of wet grass and young leaves. Lighting a fire, he piled the sodden vegetation on it. The trees were swathed in heavy drifts of smoke. There was an uneasy stirring in the branches.

'Jump!' Crow called. 'You'll be smothered if you don't get down quickly. Don't be afraid. I'll catch you.'

He held his arms wide. For a little while nothing happened. Then a plump body hurtled through the smoke towards his outstretched arms. At the last moment Crow stepped aside. The body fell and was impaled on the bone.

Ignoring its cries and struggles, Crow picked it up and carried it to the fire, holding it over the billowing smoke. The blood that dripped from its torn body quickly congealed. The creature writhed in his arms. From the shapeless flesh, amorphous protrusions gradually assumed their final shape. Crow looked at the body which had been so ungainly and even repellent, marvelling at the delicacy of its features, at the sparkling eyes that looked into his, the long lashes, the broad nose and prominent lips, ears more delicate and exquisite than any fragile seashell, body and limbs rounded, soft, and inviting, feet that could walk the endless plains and hands and fingers that seemed made for food-gathering, fire-lighting, and the work he would require from a wife.

She was the first woman, at least of the tribe of the Eagle-hawk, and he the first man of the Crow family. For Crow there arose new obligations from that day—the need to protect her, to hunt for them both, and the final responsibility of fatherhood.*

---

* The myth offers an explanation of the relationship between Crow and Eagle-hawk moieties.

There is some connection between totemic ancestors and the creation of the first men and women. Not infrequently it is the ancestor of a particular totem (whether man or woman) who is the subject of individual myths.

Amongst the tribes of the Murray River the Crow again appears, not as the progenitor but as the agent by which a woman ancestress appears on the scene.

In the Murray River myth, Crow wished to cross the river. As he was unable to swim the only way to get to the far side was to construct a canoe. This proved more difficult than he thought. He searched up and downstream looking for a suitable tree to provide the hull of a bark canoe. Some were too small. Or the bark was too thin. Or there was some hole or defect that would let the water through. When at last he did find a suitable tree it was at some distance from the river. Painstakingly he cut the bark with his knife and stripped off a large sheet, sewing the ends and placing spreaders to shape it to his liking.

Placing it on his head, he set off in the direction of the river. He had not gone far before he heard a rhythmic tapping sound. It was too regular to have any natural origin. He kept on walking, his eyes darting to right and left, trying to probe the undergrowth in search of the noise-maker who was apparently accompanying him. As the sound neither rose nor fell in intensity, he came at last to the conclusion that it must be coming from the canoe.

He lowered it to the ground and looked inside. To his surprise he saw a woman sitting in it. Crow had never seen a member of the opposite sex. He sat down and stared at her, fascinated by the anatomical differences. The woman spoke no word. When he stood up, she stepped out of the canoe and helped him carry it to the bank of the river and launch it.

Crow was coming to the conclusion that this strange, silent being had been providentially placed there simply to help him. He handed her the paddle but, to his further surprise, she shook her head vigorously and took her place in the canoe, evidently expecting him to do the hard work of paddling across the river.

It was the beginning of a long series of lessons that the bachelor Crow was to learn about the relationship between man and woman, and their individual responsibilities. Some of the lessons were hard to learn, but there were compensations,

94

and sharing of many of the tasks he had had to perform before he met the woman.

In time they settled down to a working partnership, each with his or her own duties. Two children were born, each of a different totem. For protection against danger, the mother kept them hidden in a tree; but one day, when both parents were away from the encampment, the children scrambled down from their perch. Once they reached the ground they took on human form and became the earliest Aboriginals from whom all others are descended.

The Kurnai tribe, which lives in the eastern coastal districts of Victoria, substitutes the Pelican for the Crow, and identifies his woman as Tuk, the Musk-duck.

The Death of Man

THE advent of death is no less mysterious and awe-inspiring than that of birth. The beliefs that centred round the final destiny of man were as varied as those that explained how he was first created. In some areas the fear of visitation by the ghosts of those who were once living men and women were very real, giving rise to involved burial ceremonies. There were divergent accounts of spirit worlds, and of the spirits of human beings being translated to the sky world as stars. There were beliefs in rebirth in subsequent generations. And among some tribes there was certainly the belief that death was final and irrevocable, with no hope of an afterlife. It was a fate that eventually overtook even the most vigorous and powerful totemic ancestor who, after arduous journeying, was destined to end his days as a pile of rocks, or as sacred emblems. While the ancestor might, and usually did, achieve rebirth, it was in lesser mortal form, bereft of the power and endurance that won him fame.

For mortal man, the final annihilation, even though it might be delayed, could never be avoided. In *Aranda Traditions*, Professor Strehlow tells that among some Aranda subtribes the souls of the dead take a journey to the Island of the Dead in the northern seas, where they are destroyed by bolts of lightning;

that others pay visits to their graves before their destruction; that others again are confined to lifeless but sacred tjurunga. 'But none of these varying versions has any comforting power in the face of death itself; the native has no hope of future life in which he himself will rejoin his friend, his kindred, his family, or any of those who were once dear to him.'

The Aranda legend of the Curlews of Ilkakngara provides an explanation of the origin of this belief.

First came the Curlew women, one by one, from an opening in the rocks. Many women came, and after them the Curlew men, one by one, from the same opening, until the last one emerged.

The women were glad that they had been followed by their menfolk, but the men were angry. Their anger was directed against their leader, the first to come out of the rock.

'Why did he follow the women so closely?' they asked. 'Why did he take the lead? Why did he not let us come out together? Is it because he wanted first choice of the women?'

These and other questions were bandied about, adding fuel to their indignation. The women said nothing. They stood in a circle, eyeing the men speculatively, as women sometimes do when men are not looking.

The man who had emerged first from the rock took no notice of them nor of the women. He busied himself lighting a fire, thinking to please everyone by providing warmth for those who, like himself, had endured the age-long chill of a rock-bound prison. His thoughtfulness was ill-rewarded. After conferring among themselves, the men chose one of their number to point the bone that brings death.

And so the first man of all men was the first to die. His body was racked with pain for a moment. Then, the brief convulsion over, he lay in the cold sleep of death, unwarmed by the fire he had lit for those he believed were his friends.

The women danced slowly and sadly round his body, grieving for the one who had loved them, until they were driven away by the men.

The body was buried in the stony soil, and the men clustered round the fire. Presently one of them shouted in alarm, pointing to the spot where they had buried the dead man. The ground above the buried body was heaving as though some subterranean animal was trying to come to the surface. Two large stones fell outwards, followed by a hillock of earth seamed with runnels of sliding sand and tiny particles of earth. With horrid fascination they watched as a shock of human hair, followed by a face with wide, staring eyes issued from between the tip-tilted stones. Nose, mouth, chin and neck were plainly visible. It was the head of their leader, the one they had killed and buried, come to life again.

They shrank back, fearing the vengeance of one who had the power to rise unharmed from the grave. They waited for his body to follow, but his shoulders remained below ground. Only the head moved, the eyes shifted from one to another, and the mouth opened to speak words of reproach or condemnation. Unknown to those who watched, the man's shoulders were caught under the stones, preventing him from rising further.

Suddenly the men were thrown aside. Urbura the Magpie rushed through the crowd, scattering the men like leaves in a passing gust of wind. In his hand he held a heavy spear. He thrust the barbed point deep into the man's neck, withdrew it and stamped fiercely on the man's head, forcing it into the ground with blow after blow.

As it disappeared the boulders rolled back, covering the hollow, sealing head and body beneath them.

The women crept nearer, still chanting their mournful song, stamping their feet as Urbura had stamped his.

'Stay fast, held for ever!' Urbura shouted. 'Do not try to rise! Stay in the grave for ever!'

Urbura the Magpie spread newly-sprouted wings and took flight, followed by the men and women, now changed to curlews who shriek and wail when they remember the death and dying again of the first curlew.

Had Urbura not killed him a second time, death would not have come to mankind. In the words of Professor Strehlow's informant, 'and now all of us die and are annihilated for ever; and there is no resurrection for us'.

Strehlow assures us that the idea expressed in these words is 'entirely dissociated from any Christian teachings'.

Again, there is a Murray River myth that tells of Nooralie, the Great Spirit, who created order out of chaos in the heavens and on earth. Men and women were not differentiated by sex, so far as their physical features were concerned. Animals were a queer mixture, and in the sky, sun, moon, and stars pursued an aimless course.

With the assistance of Bonelya the Bat, Nooralie tidied up the disordered elements of nature. When his work was finished the whole world became as we know it, with one exception. Death had not come to men and women.

Bonelya crawled into a hollow tree and fell into a deep sleep. Concerned for his faithful helper, Nooralie warned men and women not to come near him until he was fully rested. Some time later a woman happened to pass by. She was carrying a load of firewood and accidentally knocked it against the tree. The hollow trunk boomed like a drum, waking Bonelya, who crawled out and flew away.

Nooralie was so annoyed that his faithful friend had been disturbed that he brought death to men and women as the final act of creation.

Amongst the Kulin people it was said that at first the Moon revived those who died with a drink of magic water, thus prolonging their lives indefinitely. For some reason the Pigeon disapproved of the practice. Exercising his own considerable talents, he counteracted the effect of the magic water, so that those who died remained dead—as men have done ever since. The only one who survived the superior magic of Pigeon was Moon himself who, when on the point of death, is revived and comes to life once more each month.

While it was held by some that death was final and irrevocable, in many parts of the continent there was a variety of beliefs in a continuing state of existence. Many of these have been summarised by R. M. and C. H. Berndt in *The World of the Australians*.* The Lower Murray tribes say that when the culture hero Ngurunderi completed his journey among men, he took his sons with him on a long trek to the land of the dead, somewhere to the west. On the way one of his sons went missing, leaving one of his spears behind him. Ngurunderi tied a

---

* The writer is indebted to the authors for the information that follows.

rope to the butt of the spear and threw it, in the expectation that it would find its way to the missing boy. It found its owner. The lad caught hold of it and was drawn back into the company of his father and brothers.

Ever since then the souls of the dead are drawn up to their final home, where they are received with kindness. Infirmities they may have suffered during their life on earth are healed, and those who were aged are given renewed youth and vigour, and supplied with husbands or wives. There is no sadness in that world. Many who come there grieve at first for those they have left behind, but before long they feel at home in their new existence.

It is said that before his departure Ngurunderi dived into the sea near Kangaroo Island, and that the spirits of the dead follow the path he pioneered by crossing first to the island and cleansing themselves as he did.

The sky is the traditional spirit home of many tribes, many of which have a recognised point of departure or jumping off place. At Botany Bay there is an invisible tree that provides a bridge from this world to the spirit land. In order to reach the far side, various tests must be passed. Elsewhere the departing spirit climbs a rope to the land in the sky where Baiame is waiting to receive it. In this case the tests are severe, but with what a European might regard as a tinge of humour. To the Aboriginal they had deeper significance. Having climbed the rope, the spirit must then pass through two revolving rocks which, as they turn, reveal the Moon god and the Sun goddess who are endowed with sexual characteristics of abnormal size. The more timid souls dare not pass by, but those who are bold pass between them unharmed.* Before entering the Sky-land and being received by Baiame, a spirit must endure a series of questions by two ancestors without replying. Finally it is forced to watch erotic dances and listen to women singing humorous and no doubt suggestive songs without reacting to them. It would seem, therefore, that the spirit world is denied to those

---

* There would seem to be some affinity here with the attempt made by the Polynesian demigod Maui to overcome Hine-nui-o-te-po, the goddess of death, by passing through her body. He failed in the attempt, and so was unsuccessful in overcoming death.

who retain the carnal appetites of the life they have abandoned, and that only the pure in mind are admitted to the celestial abode!

The destiny of the spirits who fail the tests is not stated, but it may be assumed that they remain on earth, either to linger by their bones, or to plague the living. In some places men and women are supposed to be possessed of two or more spirits, one of which is received into a paradisean afterlife, the others remaining behind as malicious ghosts.

In western Arnhem Land the departed spirit has to endure many tribulations before being admitted to Manidjirangamad, the Sky-land. An unpleasant individual named Gunmalng knocks out its teeth with a club. If the gums bleed the spirit is sent back to its body, for death has not yet come to its owner. A bloodless spirit continues its journey, but has to avoid a guardian who is waiting with his spear. Fortunately a protector is at hand. The first sign that this peril is being approached is the presence of a white cockatoo, which screams to announce the coming of one who is striving to reach Manidjirangamad. Thus warned, the guardian's wife offers to remove the lice from her husband's hair. If the spirit is sufficiently wary and agile it will be able to steal past the guardian without being seen. In order to protect herself, the woman waits until the spirit is at a safe distance before telling the guardian that she has seen it. It is then too late for him to catch up with it.

The perils of the road are not yet over. The spirit comes to a group of people who are eating fish, while nearby a second guardian is waiting to cut off its legs. As soon as they see it the people begin crying piteously to arouse the guardian. On being told that they want more fish, he rolls over and goes to sleep, and the spirit is able to steal past unnoticed.

Finally the spirit comes to a river which can be crossed only by canoe. If it is a male spirit, the ferryman conveys it to the other side in an old canoe, beating it with a club or paddle all the way across. If the spirit is female, the ferryman provides a new canoe and treats the ghostly woman courteously, but expects payment in the manner that men so often demand of women.

If, after surviving the hazards of the road to Manidjirangamad, the spirit arrives at its destination, it is sure of a welcome by its ghostly inhabitants.

In the legends of most ethnic races in the Southern Hemisphere there are usually accounts of visits paid to the land of the dead by mortals. A number of these tales have been extant amongst Aboriginals.*

To the people of Arnhem Land the island of Bralgu is the land of the dead, where spirits dance the endless years away. One of their occupations is to send the morning star to the northern coasts. To do this, they tie balls composed of feathers to a large pole by means of strings. The balls are thrown out into the night sky, where they shine like stars. When morning comes the balls are retrieved by pulling in the strings—a ritual practice repeated by the Aboriginals in the mortuary ritual of the Morning Star.

A man named Jalngura of Bremer Island noticed that a yam leaf had dropped by his side. As a strong wind was blowing from the island of Bralgu he knew that it must have been wafted from the spirit land and, on the spur of the moment, decided to visit that fabled island while he was still a man and bring back word of what he had been able to see.

It took several days hard paddling in his canoe before he reached Bralgu. He stepped ashore, carrying a spear-thrower which was a replica of those he believed to be made by the spirits. It was cylindrical in shape, adorned at one end with human hair.

When the spirits saw that he was carrying a Bralgu woomera they accepted him as one of themselves, greeting him as a new arrival and providing him with a feast of yams. When night came he was entertained with dances and provided with clapping sticks with which to keep time. In return he sang to them, and was rewarded with three attractive girls, who became his wives.

Before dawn they wakened him and invited him to observe the rite of the Morning Star. This was what Jalngura longed to see. He was taken to an old woman who kept the balls of seagull feathers in a basket. Of all the spirit men and women he had met, she was the only one who harboured a suspicion that he might not be what he pretended. She refused to take the balls

---

* See also *Aboriginal Fables*, which contains an account of the quest of Baiame by Yooneeara.

out of the container while he was present. No amount of pleading by other spirits would make her change her mind until Jalngura begged her to show them to him and sang a magic song that persuaded her to cooperate.

When the balls were taken out Jalngura was surprised and yet relieved to see that they were exactly the same as those used by his people in their own ceremonies. He watched, fascinated, as they were tossed out on the ends of their feathered strings and gleamed with steady flame in the pale light of dawn.

As the old woman pulled at the strings in order to restore the balls to the receptacle in which they were kept, Jalngura begged her never to cease heralding the coming of day with these comforting lights.

She looked at him from under lowered brows.

'That I shall do, whether you ask me or not, mortal,' she said. 'You are here under false pretences. If it were not that you had charmed me with your song there would be no place for you here or on your own island. I fear you will pay for your rashness. In your turn you must promise me one thing. When you return to the land of Bralgu, as you must, whether soon or late, promise me that you will bring your wives and children with you.'

Jalngura promised readily and with a light heart got into his canoe and sped back to Bremer Island, where he had many things to tell to his fellows.

That night he chose one of his wives to lie with—and the prophecy of the keeper of the Morning Star came true. The long and strenuous double voyage in his canoe had weakened his back. In the night it broke and before he could wake to see the Morning Star again, his spirit and that of his wives and children were again on the way to the land of Bralgu.

River and Sea

Two brothers named Malgaru and Jaul lived near the Centre. After a long period without rain the water holes and soaks were all dry. Malgaru had foreseen the drought and prepared for it by sewing up a kangaroo skin and filling it with water. Once the waterholes ran dry Malgaru refused to share the water with the improvident Jaul, which led to bitterness between the brothers. Jaul realised that if he were to survive he must leave his own territory and seek water elsewhere. His brother agreed and offered to accompany him.

When they arrived at Biranbura, near Fowlers Bay, they searched for pools without success. Malgaru placed his water bag in the shade cast by some rocks before going farther afield to look for food and water. During his absence Jaul, maddened by thirst, burst the bag. The water gushed out and ran across the sand. Malgaru saw what was happening. He ran back in an attempt to save what he could, but was too late to prevent a different kind of catastrophe. The water continued to pour out of the bag, filling the hollows, spreading inland, and into a deep depression that is now part of the sea.

Both the brothers were drowned in the flood. When the birds saw the torrent that threatened to inundate the whole country and destroy the trees that supplied them with berries, they began to build a dam to hold back the flood waters. The only materials they could find were roots of the kurrajong tree. Because of the use made of them on that tragic day the tree is sometimes called the water tree. In later years it proved a boon to the Aboriginals, for it flourished for longer than other trees in time of drought. Its roots contained water that could be expressed to provide a supply for drinking. The reason is that the water that came from the kangaroo skin bag soaked into them when they were used as a dam to prevent the flood from engulfing the inland plains.

Long before there was any Murray River, long before Ngurunderi made his journey along its banks, a small family group camped at Swan Hill. There were six members in this tiny clan, Totyerguil the father, two Black Swan wives known as Gunewarra, two sons, and Totyerguil's mother-in-law Yerrerdet-kurrk. They were all dependent on the hunter's skill.

While the Gunewarra were preparing the evening meal, Totyerguil told his sons to collect a supply of gum. They had only just arrived and their camp was in unfamiliar territory. Before long the boys came running back in a state of excitement.

'There's a big waterhole over there,' they gasped. 'And in it there's an enormous fish—the biggest fish we've ever seen.'

Totyerguil was sceptical. Most of his life having been spent in mallee country where there were only small soaks, he had seldom seen fish of any kind.

'How big?' he asked.

'Big as this! Bigger!' they said, spreading their arms to their fullest extent. 'Much, much bigger!'

Their father accompanied them to the waterhole, which he found to be a pond many metres across. There was no sign of the fish that his sons said had been lying near the surface, its back appearing like a small island in the pool. Totyerguil peered down into the depths of the pool where, much to his surprise, he could discern the shadowy form of what was undoubtedly a monster fish.

'Spear it!' the boys shouted, but their father shook his head.

'It's too far down, too far away from the bank,' he said. 'I must make a canoe so I can spear it from above. Come and help me.'

He cut the bark from a nearby tree and sewed the ends roughly together.

'That will do,' he told his sons. 'It's not a very good canoe but it will keep afloat long enough for me to get at the fish.'

Gathering his spears, he got gingerly into his homemade canoe and paddled quietly across the pool until he was directly above the sleeping fish. Raising his arm he drove the spear through the water and thrust it deep into the fish's back.

The boys, who were standing on the bank, saw the canoe lifted up as though by a tidal wave. The still water broke into waves that dashed over the bank, smashing into each other, sending spouts of water high into the air. The canoe, with Totyerguil clinging desperately to the frail bark, was lost to sight in the heaving cauldron. The boys feared that their father would be drowned or swallowed by the great fish, but when the tumult of water subsided they saw that the canoe was still afloat, though practically waterlogged, and their father was still clinging doggedly to it with one hand and holding his remaining spears in the other.

Far below the surface of the pool the fish, which we are told was Otchout, the father of all Murray cod, broke out of the pool that had long been his home. Like a battering ram, it dashed head-first into the bank and then up to the surface. The walls of the tunnel he made fell in. Water rushed into the channel, sweeping the canoe along with it.

All that day Otchout fled from the spear-throwing Totyerguil, who was borne on the crest of the wave that raced along the trench.

Night fell. By this time the fisherman had been left far behind. He camped for the night, enduring cold and hunger, while Otchout rested comfortably in a deep pool he had excavated with his fins. The spear, which remained upright in his back, troubled him, but he was confident that, having left the hunter behind, he would be able to dispose of it.

Long before sun-up Totyerguil was awake and on the trail again. Arriving at the second pool just as the first shafts of sunlight lit the horizon, he hurled a spear at Otchout. It landed immediately behind the one he had thrown the previous day.

Once again the startled cod hurled itself against the bank and fled across the land, excavating the unending trench along which the water rushed headlong, with Totyerguil trying to keep pace by paddling furiously. When night fell, the fish was again far ahead; and again it made a hole in which to rest, while the hunter spent another fireless, foodless night in the open.

Day after day, Totyerguil followed Otchout, night after night they rested, and each following morning or night another spear was planted in the fish's back.

At Murray Bridge, where the white man threw a bridge across the river a hundred years ago, Otchout made his last pool and Totyerguil threw his last spear. The hunt was over. Otchout's back bristled with spears, which we can still see as the spines of the Murray cod. The river we call Murray was made, increasing in volume as it was fed by rain and various tributaries, flowing gently until it reached the sea more than a hundred kilometres distant. Otchout was translated into a star, while the disappointed hunter set out on foot to return to his family at Swan Hill.

Before he left he dragged his battered canoe ashore and planted a pole he had made from the branch of a Murray pine upright beside it. The bark canoe took root and grew into a gigantic gum tree. The paddle pole became the prototype of all the canoe paddles made by the tribesmen of the Murray River district in later years.

When Totyerguil arrived at the camping ground at Swan Hill, he found it deserted. He had been away so long that his family had given him up as dead.

The fish had grown night after night, as the boys told and re-told of the way it had struggled when it was speared by their father.

'He must have been swallowed whole,' Yerrerdet-kurrk said. 'It's no use waiting for him to come back from the fish's stomach. We've got to find a better campsite than this. The pool is drained. We'll find no more fish there, I can tell you, and you boys aren't skilled hunters like your father. We'll have to try some other place.'

They left their camp and went eastwards.

Although they had long been gone, Totyerguil was able to follow their trail. It led across the plains, into the foothills, and then up steep mountain sides, until at last he came to the blank wall of a cliff. He looked round in every direction. As there was no sign of their passing on the stony ground, he wondered whether they had been killed and eaten by some monster from the mountains. As a last resort he shouted, 'Are you there? I am Totyerguil. Are you there, my wife? Are you there, my sons?'

The words echoed among the ravines, diminishing to a last faint 'Are you there? there? there?'

To his surprise he heard a reply from far above. 'Yes, we're here, here, here.'

Somehow the two women and two young men had managed to scramble up the steep mountain sides. Having reached the top, they found themselves unable to get back. Totyerguil had arrived in time, before they perished of starvation and cold.

'You must throw yourselves down,' the hunter shouted. 'Don't be afraid. I'll catch you. You won't hurt yourselves.'

Summoning up courage, his youngest wife threw herself from the cliff top and was caught in the arms of her husband. She was followed by the older wife, and then by the two boys, who enjoyed the sensation of hurtling through the air.

Last of all came the old woman, Yerrerdet-kurrk. Totyerguil spread his arms instinctively, but at the last moment he remembered that it was forbidden for a man to speak to or even look at his mother-in-law.*

The poor woman crashed to the ground, breaking several bones, which took some time to heal. While they were mending, the family was forced to remain at the foot of the mountain. Hunting was poor, and Totyerguil had to venture far afield in search of game, as also did his wives, searching for grubs and other insects and what little vegetable food they could find. This they all did ungrudgingly, but the old lady harboured resentment against her son-in-law. She suspected that he had drawn back on purpose instead of catching her in his arms; even if that were not true, he might have ignored the tribal law for the sake of saving her from possible death.

Once she recovered, the hunter led them all on a journey that took many days, and ended in a pleasant place where there was plenty of water, with trees, and yams, and other plants, and an abundant supply of game. For a while they all lived happily together.

The old woman concealed her feelings. She had not forgotten her grievance, and was only waiting until memory of the accident had gone from the minds of others. Revenge, when it came, would be even sweeter for the delay. She was in no hurry. She would know when the time was ripe.

During this period Totyerguil did not set up a permanent camp site. He wanted to explore the whole region before settling in one place, spending some time at each stopping place.

In her search for yams Yerrerdet-kurrk came one day to a deep waterhole. In skirting it she saw a bunyip lurking in its depths. A plan formed in her mind. She visited the pool several times, bringing branches and sticks of wood which she piled on the bank. Each time she came she looked into the pool to see if the bunyip was awake. It looked up at her with its wicked eyes,

---

* It was an almost universal rule that once a man was betrothed he had no further converse with his future wife's mother. Amongst some tribes they were not permitted to speak to each other under any circumstances, but only through a third person. In some cases a special language or vocabulary was employed. In others sign language was used. It was customary for the woman to turn away when she saw her son-in-law or heard him speaking. The tabu did not create ill feeling. When she was in need she looked to him for help.

and she drew back quickly. The day came when the bunyip was asleep—but Totyerguil was away hunting. She began to fear they would shift camp before the presence of her son-in-law coincided with one of the bunyip's occasional sleeping spells.

But at last the day came. There was a plentiful supply of meat. Totyerguil had decided to straighten and oil his spears and lash the heads more firmly to the shaft. With a fast-beating heart Yerrerdet-kurrk floated her collection of timber and leafy branches over the water, spreading them so thickly that there was no sign of the hole. She ran back to the camp and called to her son-in-law, 'Come quick. I've found the nest of a bandicoot.'

Seeing the piles of leaves and branches, he thought that it must indeed be the nest of a bandicoot. He advanced towards it cautiously, holding a spear in one hand and a boomerang in the other.

His mother's brother, Collenbitchik the Bull-ant, who had joined the family some time before, came running up to see what all the excitement was about. Yerrerdet-kurrk caught him by the arm and said urgently, 'Tell your nephew not to use his spears.'

'Why not?'

'It would spoil the flesh. The best way is for him to jump on the nest and catch the bandicoot with his feet. That's what my husband always did.'

'Well,' said Collenbitchik, 'I don't suppose it will make much difference. You might as well do as she says and keep her happy, Totyerguil.'

His nephew grinned. He had killed many bandicoots and knew all about their ways, but if it pleased the old woman, there seemed no harm in doing as she said.

Dropping his spear, he jumped on to the tangled branches. To his dismay he crashed through them and dropped feet first into the waterhole.

As he fell he saw the bunyip rearing up with gaping mouth and claws ready to seize him. His only weapon was his boomerang. He threw it at the hideous head, but it went wide of its mark, soared through the remains of the leafy screen and disappeared into the sky where it can now be seen as a bright star.

108

Dragged under water, Totyerguil was unable to free himself from the grasp of the bunyip and was drowned. The ripples died away. Collenbitchik, appalled by the sudden catastrophe, jumped in and dragged the body away from the monster. The mud at the bottom of the waterhole had been stirred up and he was unable to see, but he groped his way to the side, questing with his hands and fingers, which developed into the characteristic feelers of the bull-ants. So ended the life of Totyerguil whose pursuit of Otchout the Cod resulted in the formation of the Murray River.

We are told by Aldo Massola, who recorded this Wotjobaluk myth in his book *Bunjil's Cave*, that 'Totyerguil is now the star Altair, and the two smaller stars on either side of him are his two wives. His mother-in-law has become the star Rigel, and Collenbitchik's "fingers" have become the double star at the head of Capricornus.' No mention is made of the fate of the two sons, but the boomerang, Wom, is the constellation Corona Borealis.

All along the northern coast crocodile legends abound nearly as plentifully as crocodiles. From the Maung tribal territory in the Goulburn Islands comes the legend of a group of tribesmen on walkabout who came to Inimeiarwillam, near the mouth of the King River. They crossed the river by canoe, pulling it back and forth several times until they were safe on the further bank, and bestowed the name, which means 'He pulled a bark canoe'.

One man was left behind. He must have been unpopular with the others, for in spite of begging to be taken into the canoe, he was refused time after time. He finally managed to make the crossing by swimming.

'I'll turn myself into a crocodile,' the man said. He walked along the bank until he came to a grove of ironwood trees. Digging up some of the roots, he heated them over a fire, peeled off the bark, and pounded them on a flat stone until they were soft enough to be moulded by hand. When he was satisfied with the shape he placed it on his nose, elongating it until it looked like the long, flattened snout of a crocodile. As he slid across the muddy bank, his body grew long, a tail formed at the base of his spine, his skin hardened into scale-like armour, his legs and arms shrank, thickened, and ended in claws. Wicked teeth protruded from his jaws. He had changed from man into crocodile.

Silently he swam downstream, his eyes protruding above water, with the rest of his body concealed. He was delighted to find that he was not too late. The canoe was making its last journey. Rearing up, he opened his jaws wide, seized the canoe in his teeth, and shook it, spilling the frightened tribespeople into the stream.

With frantic strokes they attempted to swim to the shore, encouraged by the shouts of their friends who were safe on the bank. The metamorphosed man-crocodile was too quick for them. With strong strokes of his tail, he darted from one to another, his teeth coming together with a vicious snap, tearing them limb from limb, until all that remained were severed limbs and mutilated bodies drifting out to sea in the reddened water.

His revenge was short-lived, for he was snatched away from the scene of carnage and placed high in the heavens. His position there, where he can do no harm to mortals, is indicated by three stars, with another three to show where the bark canoe has been placed. In it were three young women. They did not escape the man-crocodile's fury, but are now represented by three lumps at the back of every crocodile's head and are supposed to warn the reptiles of coming danger.

In *Aboriginal Legends* there is a story that tells of the fate of Pikuwa who seduced two girls and was trapped by them in a pit. In a variant of the legend Bindagbindag (for that was the name given to him by the Ngulugongga of the Daly River) was a man who pursued his own daughters who had taken refuge high in the branches of a banyan tree. Bindagbindag swarmed up a rope that had been left dangling from the tree house. When he neared the top his wife sawed through it with a sharpened mussel shell and he fell to the ground.

For many days and nights he lay there. All his bones were broken and he was unable to move. When they began to mend he was aware that he had lost the resemblance of a man, for his limbs were splayed out in all directions.

'I am no longer a man,' he said sadly. 'I shall make my home in the water. It will buoy me up and I shall no longer feel pain when I move.'

110

He crept to the edge of the bank and slid into the slowly moving water. It cradled him and the pain slowly ebbed away.

'Now I am neither man nor any other creature,' he said. 'I am more crocodile than man. I can never return to my former state and as I am, it will be difficult to feed myself. There's only one thing left to do. I must turn into a crocodile.'

The change, as related in the legend of the crocodile of Inimeiarwillam, came quickly. To try out his powers he snapped at a dog that was swimming close by and had the satisfaction of feeling his teeth crunch through flesh and bones.

He, too, was translated to the Sky-land, with all his family. The rope from which he fell is the Milky Way and a dark hole the banyan tree, with his wife and daughters camped under it, safely protected from his shining teeth.

The Frilled Lizard

FIFTY kilometres north of Cape York is an island named Nelgi, which was once occupied by lizards, goannas, and snakes, their leader being a Frilled Lizard called Walek.

Fire was unknown to the early inhabitants of the islands of Torres Strait, who placed their food on sun-warmed stones and cooked it a little at a time. It was a prolonged, time-consuming process. Far away from the coastal islands of New Guinea they often saw smoke rising, and suspected that their relatives had found some way of cooking their food properly.

At a tribal meeting Karum, the Monitor Lizard, was asked to find out whether this was true. He slid into the water and headed north, but before long he was back again, shivering with cold.

'It's no good,' he told them. 'Cold currents came up from the bed of the sea. I was tossed about by the waves and turned from my course by the strong currents. I could barely make it back to this island of Nelgi. You must find someone who is stronger than I.'

He crawled slowly and painfully to a flat rock and lay at full length, revelling in the hot sunshine.

'Why don't you try, Walek?' asked one of the smaller lizards.

After Karum's defeat, Walek's pride was touched.

'I'll try,' he said. 'I have a sister on the mainland. She may be willing to help us.'

Before he left he told his people to watch for smoke on the northern islands as a sign that he was on his way back.

He climbed ashore at Mawat on the New Guinea coast, changed into human form, and went some distance inland where his sister, Ubu, was living. She greeted him and invited him to share their evening meal. Malek was fascinated by the sight of a fire outside the hut, and the way Ubu prepared the food by placing it on hot stones and covering it with vegetation and earth.

'Is that what is called fire?' he asked, watching the smoke and flames rising from the wood.

'Yes,' she said shortly, looking round furtively in case anyone was within earshot, for the secret of fire-making was jealously guarded by the tribe into which she had married.

'Where does it come from?'

She opened her hand and showed him four coals glowing between her fingers.

'You don't need them all. Give me one,' he begged.

She refused, but he was so persistent that she gave him one from the other hand. Malek thanked her and left at once. When he reached the water's edge he looked at the coal more closely, saw that it was black and felt cold. Realising that she had tricked him, he went back and demanded another from her right hand.

Frightened that he might do her an injury, she reluctantly parted with one of the glowing coals.

This time he changed back to his normal shape, put the coal in his mouth, and struck out strongly. On reaching Saibai, the first island he came to, he went ashore and threw the coal into some long, dry grass, which burst into flame, satisfying him that the fire was still alive.

Far to the south, on Nelgi, the reptiles were gazing anxiously across the strait, wondering whether Walek had been successful in his quest. Presently they saw a tiny thread of smoke far in the distance and, at intervals, on nearer islands as Walek kept going ashore to make sure the coal was still alight. When he arrived at his home island he was given a tumultuous welcome and soon food was being cooked and eaten with relish by everyone except Walek, whose tongue had been badly burnt, and had to be attended to for some time before he could eat. If ever one has the chance to look at the tongue of a frilled lizard, it will be seen that it bears the scar that was caused by the live coal he carried in his mouth during his long swim from New Guinea to Nelgi Island.

Sun, Moon, and Stars

THE sun is invariably regarded as female in Aboriginal legends, just as the moon is always masculine. One of the simplest and most appealing legends tells of a woman who lived in the all-pervading darkness of a world unlit by sun, moon, or stars. The only lights were the flickering bark torches held by those who were seeking food or water.

This woman, Knowee, left her small son sleeping in a cave and went out to search for yams. Without the heat of the sun to encourage plant growth there was little vegetable life on earth and it was necessary to forage far afield. She was afraid to leave the boy alone for long, lest one of the darker shapes that prowled the earth should snatch him away. But without food they would both die.

On this occasion she began to despair of finding any roots. Everywhere she went the earth was bare, broken into gorges and ravines, with huge boulders and outcrops of rock over which she was forced to climb. Growing tired in her hopeless search she decided to return to the cave. With a shock she realised that she had no idea where it was. In following one ravine that led into another, with many side passages, and guided only by the dim light of her torch, she was unable to recognise any landmark.

The only thing to do was to keep on walking, trusting that instinct would take her back to the starting point.

But alas, the farther she went the farther she wandered from the cave where her boy was lying. Weary and dispirited, she reached the very end of the world and, unknowingly, stepped from there into the dark land above the world.

Every day she traverses that vast plain, holding her torch high above her head. The flame has grown brighter with the passing of the years. In her daily march across the sky it lights up the whole world as she keeps on searching for the son who is still awaiting her return.

A Murray River tribal myth of the origin of the sun is unique in that it embodies elements of a number of separate legends that have already been related. The skilful manner in which they have been blended justifies a retelling of this extensive myth.

As in the previous story, it begins when the world was in darkness, though there must have been some kind of half-light to enable the actors in the following events to see what they were doing. It may be that earlier men and women who had been taken into the sky to shine there as stars provided the light that enabled the Emus to see how fair was the world that lay far below.

We must not be surprised at this.

The Emus were equipped with powerful wings and spent their entire lives disporting themselves above and through the clouds that wandered beneath the high dome of heaven. Not one of them had ever landed on the earth. Born in the empty space of the sky, their eggs cradled on soft clouds, with their playmates of wind and cloud, they felt no urge to explore the solid world that lay so far beneath them that it was but a blurred landscape reaching from one distant horizon to another.

Until one day, whether forced by a vagrant wind far from her aerial playground or whether by accident, a female Emu flew sufficiently close to earth to see its many features. For many hours she struggled upwards to reach her accustomed playground. On arriving there, she called her friends round her and told them, at great length, what she had seen.

'It's quite different to our home,' she said. 'Mountains and valleys don't change their shape as they do here. But the colours! Beautiful greens and browns, and greys, silver and gold, crimson flowers of every shape and size! Clouds of leaves blowing in the wind—and things that move on two legs and four. Some with wings but most without, climbing the mountains, swimming in rivers and lakes. If only the light had been brighter I would have seen more.'

Her friends thought she was romancing.

'It can't be like this world of ours,' they said. 'See how we fly through the changing clouds that are never the same from one day to another. You can have that dull, petrified world if you want it. This is the home that Baiame has given us. You should be ashamed to want to go to one where you don't belong.'

Emu hid behind a cloud and sulked. 'They don't understand,' she said to herself. 'If they'd seen it as I have, they'd want to go there too.'

She fell asleep, wafted to and fro on the breeze, dreaming of the new world she had seen. When she woke her mind was made up. Not waiting for the wind to blow her down, she flew joyously with strokes of her strong wings towards the earth. Sometimes she closed her wings and fell in a plummeting dive with the cold wind whistling past, smoothing the feathers close to her body. Again she opened her wings, drifting quietly, down the tenuous highways of the air, to land on a patch of green sward sheltered by tall trees.

While drifting close to the earth she was entranced by a song and the sight of heavily built birds dancing in a circle. She ran towards them, begging to be allowed to join in the dance.

One of them, a Native Companion, came up to her, keeping her wings folded close to her body.

'It is a sacred dance,' she said. 'We don't know who you are or where you have come from.'

'I am an Emu,' was the proud reply. 'I live far above you. I am the first of our tribe ever to come to your home.'

'Why have you come? Why don't you stay with your own people?'

Emu was taken aback by the rude manner of the Native Companion. It was not the kind of reception she had expected.

'Don't you want me here?' she asked. 'If I'm not wanted I'll certainly return to my tribe. I have come here because I thought everyone would be happy and kind in this beautiful world of yours.'

The Native Companion, who was jealous of Emu's mastery of the air, pretended a cordiality she was far from feeling.

'Yes, of course we'd like to have you with us,' she said sweetly. 'But there's a problem. It's those wings of yours.'

'What is the matter with them? Don't you like them?'

'Of course, of course,' Native Companion said quickly, folding her own wings even more tightly against her. 'But as I told you, this is a sacred dance. Only those birds who are wingless are allowed to join in.'

'What if I take them off?' Emu asked.

'In that case you will be welcome. Let me help you.'

She pulled with her beak and with a tearing sound the Emu's wings were removed. Standing before them, Emu was appalled at the laughter that rose from the Native Companions.

'You've been tricked,' shouted Kookaburra. 'She was jealous of your wings. You'll never be able to put them back,' and he kept on laughing, on and off, for a long time, just as his descendants do to this day.

Fortunately Emu found other friends who were better disposed towards her. She had lost the ability to fly back to her friends in the sky, but earth provided many compensations. The joy of browsing through the undergrowth, discovering new plants and succulent fruits and berries, catching frogs and fish in the billabongs with her feet in the cool water, these and a hundred other delights, and not least the freedom to join in the dances unencumbered with wings was proof that she had been wise in coming down to earth.

Nevertheless Native Companion still nourished her spiteful temper. After Emu had been some time in her new home, so long in fact that she had made a cosy nest and laid a clutch of eggs on the soft grass, Native Companion paid her a visit. She was accompanied by one fledgling, having left the others in the nest for the father bird to care for.

'Why have you got so many eggs?' she asked peering into the nest and clucking in disapproval. 'You'll have a hard job raising a brood as big as that. Much better to have one fledgling so you can give it proper attention.'

'All the women of my tribe lay several eggs,' Emu said. 'The babies are easy to look after when they break the shell.'

'In the sky, yes, where they'll never come to harm among the clouds,' was the reply, 'but not here on earth. Too many animals and reptiles here would like a tasty meal of eggs or young birds.'

The inexperienced Emu was impressed by this advice. She broke all the eggs but one and devoted herself to its care.

But the wickedness of the Native Companion did not go unpunished. Gnawdenoorte, the son of the Great Spirit, had heard what she said. He had not interfered when Emu's wings were removed, knowing that the ultimate destiny of the huge birds lay on earth and not in the sky, but at this further evidence of Native Companion's spitefulness, he took action. Two things that great man did to punish her. He changed her singing voice to a harsh croak; and, when breeding time came, her proud brood was reduced from ten or twelve to one, or at most two. The only thing he did not take from her was her graceful movements in the dance.

Emu, too, had learned her lesson—never to trust Native Companion. She was used to life on earth, seldom yearning for the freedom of the air she once possessed. Doubly so when she was joined by her husband and the friends she had known in the realm of the sky.

Another mating season came, and in due time the nest again contained its full quota of eggs. When Native Companion came drifting up to her on a day that her husband was absent, she was on guard against honeyed words. This time, the spiteful bird said nothing. Using the wings she had hidden when she had helped denude the Emu of hers, she sprang over her head, alighting on the nest, and began crushing the precious eggs with claws and beak.

Emu lashed out with her tree-like leg, sending her rolling over the ground. But Native Companion had managed to seize one of the eggs in her claw. She hurled it with all her might far into the sky, where it broke against a pile of firewood that Gnawdenoorte had prepared to warm himself. As it struck the wood, the egg burst into flame, igniting the woodpile and flooding earth and sky with light and warmth.

So the sun was born and maintains that warmth and life day after day, to the comfort of all that lives and grows on the earth below.

Bahloo, the Moon god, is usually represented as the lover of Yhi, the Sun goddess. He was a cheerful soul, fond of playing tricks on others, but never malicious. Once, long ago, he was a man who lived on earth, where he was known as Nullandi, the

Happy Man.* In old age he was raised to the sky by Baiame, where he received the new name, Bahloo, and was renewed in mind and body. Every month he declines in stature, but grows again to his full size, a sign to mankind that when they die they will be restored to life again in the land that Baiame has provided for them.

Bahloo had not long been in the sky when a terrible thing happened. The Sun goddess fell in love with him. Bahloo was still fond of the wives he had left behind and often longed to be with them again. He was frightened of Yhi, who had had many lovers, and used men as playthings. She followed him across the sky, overwhelming him with a passion that was expressed in the increased heat that emanated from her radiant body.

Bahloo hastened his steps, pursuing an erratic course that contrasted sadly with his usual slow and steady pace from east to west. As Yhi pursued him closely, he was in danger of being cornered. He fled to the edge of the sky, hoping to slide down to earth. At Yhi's command the edges were turned up, penning him like an emu caught in the net of the hunters.

It may have been the analogy that prompted him to disguise himself as an emu. He stalked past the guardians of the sky without being challenged. Arriving back on earth he went directly to the camp where he used to live and crept into his own gunyah. He prodded his wives until they woke.

'Be quiet,' he said sternly before they had time to open their mouths.

'I thought you were ...' one of the younger wives said, and then covered her mouth with her hand.

Bahloo turned to her and said, 'Yes, you thought I was—whom?'

She was reluctant to say more, but at Bahloo's insistence she confessed that his brothers had been visiting the gunyah regularly.

'Are they likely to come here tonight?'

She giggled. It was sufficient for Bahloo.

'Get up,' he said to the other wives who were lying quite still, hoping not to be drawn into the conversation.

---

* The legend of the Happy Man and Loolo the Miserable Man is related in *Myths and Legends of Australia*.

They stood up.

'Go out and fetch a large log—about this long,' he said, spreading his arms to their fullest extent. As they ran out he addressed the youngest wife.

'When they bring in the log, cover it with a kangaroo skin. Then take the others with you and hide in the bush until I call you.'

As soon as they were gone, he hid in the darkest corner of the gunyah, holding a frond of fern in front of him to disguise his unmistakable form. The waiting time was brief. He watched with some amusement as his three brothers stole in on tiptoe. His eyes were accustomed to the dark. He grinned as he saw the look of astonishment on their faces when they realised that the women were not there.

'Where are they?' one of them whispered.

'Look,' said another, 'there's someone over there in the corner, wrapped up in a kangaroo skin.'

'It must be Bahloo!' the third brother exclaimed.

They ran outside and came back with their nulla-nullas. It was with considerable enjoyment they attacked the still form, oblivious of the fact that Bahloo himself was standing in the corner thoroughly enjoying the spectacle. When the disgusted trio had left, Bahloo joined his wives and set up a new encampment, waiting until Yhi's ardour cooled, occupying his time with his favourite occupation, the manufacture of girl babies.*

Bahloo, the cheerful and often mischievous Moon god, spent a great deal of his time on earth, mainly because of the attraction of the pretty young women he found there. He was usually accompanied by his 'dogs', who were in reality snakes—which failed to endear him to the men and women he met on his lonely excursions.

On one occasion he came to a river that was so wide that he found difficulty in crossing it. He waited on the bank until a party of men came that way, and appealed to them for help.

'Will you carry my dogs across for me?' he asked.

They shrank back from him.

---

* For the legend of the making of babies, see *Aboriginal Legends*.

'No, we're frightened to touch them. They might bite us.'

'They won't hurt you,' Bahloo laughed. 'Look, I'm holding them. They don't bite me.'

When they continued to refuse, Bahloo became angry. He broke off a piece of bark and held it out.

'See this?'

He threw it into the water, where it was caught in the current and floated downstream.

'If you help me, you'll be like that piece of bark. Did you see how it disappeared and then bobbed up again? When you die you'll come to life again. Now watch this.'

He picked up a stone and tossed it into the river.

'See how it sinks? If you refuse to carry my dogs across, then you'll be like the stone. When you die, you'll never come to life again. What will you do?'

'We won't touch your dogs. We're too frightened,' they repeated.

'Very well,' said Bahloo. He picked up the snakes and swam across the river. On reaching the other side, he shouted, 'You've lost your chance. When you die you'll stay dead. You're nothing but men while you're alive, and when you're dead you'll be nothing but bones!'—and he stalked off into the bush, so angry that when the time came to make his journey across the sky, he never came back to earth again.

Another legend puts the moon in a more kindly light. Long ago men did not die because he gave them a magic drink every month to bring them back to life. It was Bronze-wing Pigeon who was the hard-hearted one. His magic was stronger than Moon's, and counteracted the magic of the water. Men who died then remained dead. Only Moon survived that superior magic and continues to revive after his death every month.

While Bahloo is the commonly accepted name of the Moon god, there are other names and legends to account for the guardian of the night sky. In a few words, a conflict between a man whose son had been killed because of misconduct between his wife and her lover resulted in both men being severely wounded. The betrayed husband drowned himself, but the lover of his wife, Japard by name, rose into the sky and became the moon man with the scars of battle plain to see on his face.

The mother of the dead boy was turned into a curlew that constantly bewails the loss of a dead husband and son.

The legend is in striking contrast to that of the cheerful Bahloo.

Every constellation and countless individual stars are productive of legends that account for their origin. Some have already been related. There is a degree of consistency in many of these tales in spite of the fact that they have come from widely separated tribal groups. The myth of the totemic ancestor or of some less distinguished figure of the Dreamtime frequently concludes with the principal actor or actors being taken into the sky to begin a new life, removed from the hazards of everyday events in the world as stars.

A typical star legend is that of the Spider Women of the Great Victoria Desert. Amongst the Spider clan that was camped by a waterhole were two sisters, one of whose duties was to take food each day to a boy who was undergoing initiation tests some distance from the encampment. They had been given strict instructions not to show themselves to him, but to light a fire as a sign that food was ready, and to hurry back to the camp.

The younger woman, intrigued by the possibility of a liaison with a man of her own age, decided that she must see him for herself. In her own words, 'I shall make myself into a wife.'

The boy was living in a hollow tree, and was safely hidden, but the next time she took food and searched for him, he was stalking a goanna. He saw her place the food on the ground and light the fire. Then, instead of leaving, she began searching for his hiding place. He bent low in order not to reveal his whereabouts and ran to the hollow tree. The Spider Woman saw his legs disappearing into the hole in the trunk. Satisfied with her discovery, she went home and told her sister what she had seen.

'You must help me,' she said. 'I want that boy for myself. When we take meat out there tomorrow, I will light the fire while you go over to the tree where he is living. Catch him for me. I'm sure he will want me when he sees me.'

Her sister agreed. On the following day, the plan was put into operation. While the younger sister was busy lighting the fire, the older one crept up to the tree. A rude ladder had been constructed to reach the opening. She cut it off and sat down to wait, hidden in the bushes. As soon as the fire was well alight, her younger sister pretended to leave, but she too concealed herself in the scrub.

It was long before the boy returned to pick up the food and take it to the hollow tree. Warned by a glimpse he had caught of the girl who had obviously been searching for him on the previous day, he waited until he was sure that the food-bearers were well away from the fire before venturing near his hiding place.

When he came to the tree he was surprised to find that the vine ladder had been removed. His suspicions aroused, he turned to run. He was too late. The elder sister sprang out of the bushes where she had concealed herself and held him tightly in her arms until the younger came running to join them.

'It's no use your trying to run away,' the older girl said. 'Anyway, why should you? My sister loves you. You should be pleased. If I let you go, will you promise not to run away?'

Seeing that there was no hope of escaping, the boy agreed. The younger sister stretched herself out on the ground, trying to persuade him to lie with her. Remembering the solemnity of the initiation rites and the penalty if he broke the prohibitions imposed by the elders, he refused to yield to her persuasions. The ordeal of the period of solitude had already been broken, which was bad in itself, even though it had not been his fault. The conviction that he must not cohabit with women during this period was so firmly impressed on him that he resisted all her blandishments.

Disgusted by his lack of cooperation, the sisters eventually left him. As he stood there, wondering what to do next, a group of other young initiates came up to him and persuaded him to go with them. Hoping he had spent sufficient time alone to satisfy the old men, the boy went with them.

They had not been gone long before the sisters returned, believing that by this time his resistance would be weakened. Finding that he had left, but puzzled by the multitude of tracks that led away from the tree, they followed them until they came to the initiation camp.

Cautiously they peeped through a screen of branches and

were in time to see the conclusion of the smoking ceremony. The boy had been held over a fire that had been piled high with green vegetation. He staggered away from it with smoke-filled lungs.

'Run!' the elder urged him. 'Run and fill your lungs with air.'

Coughing and spluttering, he ran from the fire, straight into the arms of the younger Spider Woman. Helpless to defend himself in his dazed condition, he was thrown across her shoulders and borne away. When the old men saw what frightful sacrilege was being committed, they pursued the girl, hurling spears at her. She leapt high in the air, out of reach of the flying spears, and in one tremendous bound reached the sky, where she and her reluctant husband remain for all time as twin stars.

Any recital of star legends would not be complete without mention of the constellation of the Southern Cross, which was a special creation of Baiame. It is the gum tree named Yaraan-do. The stars of the Cross are the eyes of a man and a spirit imprisoned within the tree, blazing in the darkness, while the Pointers are two white cockatoos that followed the tree when it was lifted into the sky.

Another legend gives an entirely different explanation. It goes back to the days of the Dreamtime when a vast plain was occupied by a flock of Brush Turkeys. There was much sorrow among them, for younger birds were often missed, their bones and feathers scattered among the trees and bushes being the only clue to their fate. Suspicion fell on many birds. It was only after Baiame sent two messengers that the ravisher of the flock was found to be a fierce old Turkey who had been living a solitary life on the edge of the plain.

The messengers of the Great Spirit were also Brush Turkeys of gigantic stature. They flew down to the Turkeys' camping place during a meeting that had been called to discuss the problem. After the corroboree there was a dance—and all the time the cannibal Brush Turkey was lurking behind the bushes with his eyes on a young Turkey girl.

In the small hours of the morning, when the dancers lay down to rest, the old-man Turkey stole into the circle and picked up the youngster he had selected as the tenderest and juiciest of all the young ones. As he was on the point of disappearing into a thicket he looked up and saw a huge bird towering over him. A moment later old-man Turkey was lying on his back, half stunned, looking up with an expression of dismay on his old wrinkled face. Another great bird stood over him, there was the soft sound of a second blow, and the cannibal lay dead on the rim of the dancing floor.

When daylight came and the birds got sleepily to their feet, Baiame's messengers told them what had happened during the night.

'That is the end of your troubles,' they said. 'Your children will never be molested again.'

They gobbled and clucked with relief. From their midst the two celestial birds rose into the air, flapping their wings, mounting swiftly towards the sky, where Baiame rewarded them by placing them as Pointers to the Cross for all men—and turkeys—to admire for ever.

The Insect Tribe

ONE of the great mysteries of the Dreamtime was that of death. Belief in the finality of death and the alternative of an afterlife have already been mentioned. It was the tribe of butterflies that provided comfort to those who were ready to accept that their experience was symbolic of an afterlife for beings whose days, whether short or long, would find fulfilment beyond the grave.

Long before men came to Australia, when the only occupants of the land were various forms of animal life and death had not yet entered the world, it was the habit of their representatives to gather once a year on the banks of the Murray River.

As they were able to talk to each other, the nights were spent discussing the enigma of life. In the midst of such a gathering a white feathered form crashed into the centre of the circle. It was a cockatoo that had been craning its neck, trying to overhear the conversation of the old men, and had overbalanced. The bird was old and decrepit. Caught unawares, it had no time to open its wings before it struck the ground.

The old men looked at it in consternation. Getting to their feet they bent over the body, but could detect no sign of life. Never in all their experience had they witnessed death in any form. The services of the medicine-men were secured, but the body of the bird grew stiff and cold and even the most skilled of the clever-men were unable to revive it.

When they had assured themselves there was no sign of life in the cockatoo, the discussion grew animated.

Life they could understand but not this strange absence of life that imposed an invisible barrier against the activity, motion, and intelligence they had experienced without question. They knew that new life came from the spirits sent by the ancestors, but where did this strange state of non-being come from? Where did the spirit that controlled the body go?

Finding no answer to these questions, the following day all the animals, including birds, reptiles, and insects, were called together to see if anyone could provide the answer. Mopoke, who had the reputation of being the wisest of the birds, was asked. He blinked his eyes solemnly but refused to speak.

It was Eagle-hawk, the leader of the bird clan, who contributed a positive statement. He picked up a pebble and threw it into the river, looking round for approval. No one moved or spoke.

'Don't you understand?' Eagle-hawk asked when the silence became oppressive. 'You saw the pebble when I held it up. Now it has gone into the river. Vanished from your sight. It has gone. It is no more. There is no pebble. That is what has happened to the spirit of Cockatoo. Yesterday it was alive in his body. Now it has gone, leaving only his flesh and blood and feathers. Throw them into the river and Cockatoo will be no more, as the pebble is no more.'

Still there was no reply. He had not succeeded in convincing them.

Then Crow stepped forward, holding another pebble in his claw. They leaned forward to hear what he had to say. Though many of them had suffered from his practical jokes, everyone recognised that he had an ingenious mind and might have a solution to this puzzling question.

He hopped on to a ledge of rock and threw his pebble into the river. It went in with a plop that everyone could hear. Crow went back to his former position without speaking, and again silence fell. When no one ventured to open his mouth, Crow clattered his beak impatiently.

'The answer is obvious. The pebble is still a pebble. We can't see it, because it's on the bed of the river. If you don't believe me, Frog will dive down to bring it up and show you.'

'Yes, it must be there,' they said in chorus.

'Very well, you stupid animals. Eagle-hawk thinks his pebble has vanished because he can't see it, but I say that it is still a pebble, in a new element. It's now a water-pebble instead of a land-pebble, isn't it?'

'Yes, yes.'

'Well, that is what has happened to Cockatoo's spirit. It's still a spirit, but it's no longer in his body. He's dead, but his spirit is alive, somewhere. We can't see it. We couldn't see it when he was alive, could we? Now it's in another place. Perhaps it's in another body. Maybe Baiame has sent a mouse, or a rat, or a wombat, or a kangaroo, or even an eagle-hawk,' he said, looking at Eagle-hawk slyly.

Eagle-hawk ruffled his feathers angrily.

'Let me hit you on the head and send your spirit away,' he said. 'If you're so sure that it will still be alive, then you'll be able to come back again.'

'No,' said Crow calmly. 'I know where the pebbles are, but unless someone brings them back, they'll stay in their underwater world. I wouldn't like that to happen to me. And if I did come back, it might be in another animal like a worm—or a lizard, or even an eagle-hawk, which would be worst of all.'

'Then you're not ready to prove what you've been saying?'

'Yes, I think I am,' Crow said slowly, 'but not in the way you want.'

He raised his voice so that everyone could hear.

'It will soon be winter when many of us go to sleep until the warm weather returns. Others, like many of my friends the birds, fly away away in search of the sun. During the long winter months, let the animals and the reptiles who go to sleep see if they can change into another body and show us what they look like when they come back here in the spring. And the same with those who go away. Then we shall find out whether their spirits enter into a new life.'

126

After some discussion it was agreed that Crow's experiment was worth a trial. Eagle-hawk was about to dismiss the gathering when a chorus of their voices seemed to come from beneath his feet.

'What about us?' they called. 'May we try too?'

'Who are you? Where are you?' Eagle-hawk asked.

A small caterpillar stood on his hind segments, reaching up as far as he could.

'I represent the insects,' he squeaked. 'The bugs and the beetles, the worms and the caterpillars. We want to see what happens to our spirits.'

'I didn't know you had spirits,' Eagle-hawk said scornfully. 'I'm afraid I didn't see you down there. You can't be much use to us, but if you want to try I suppose there's no harm in that.'

The corroboree was over. Some of the furry animals prepared their burrows for the long cold nights of winter. The migratory birds left for their winter quarters. Before long only the hardier animals and birds stayed behind to forage for food in the cheerless days ahead.

Of the insects there was little sign. They had hidden in crevices in trees and rocks, burrowed beneath the soil, hidden under water, or attached themselves to trees and wrapped themselves in cocoons.

The winter months passed slowly. The days increased in length. The sun warmed the ground. The trees fluttered their leaves in anticipation of the soft winds of spring. One by one animals emerged from their winter quarters, or flew southwards towards the meeting place.

Eagle-hawk called them together and addressed Crow.

'Let's see the new forms of your coming-back-to-life spirits,' he jeered. 'Here's Wombat. He looks the same to me as he did when we were last here. Maybe he's brushed his coat, and not before time. And here's Snake. I see he's got a new skin and he looks bigger than before, but really, Crow, he's still the same old Snake.'

Crow looked round doubtfully. Some of the animals sniggered. Kookaburra let out an ear-shattering laugh in which others joined.

Suddenly Crow shouted at the top of his voice, 'Be quiet! See what's coming!'

A broad stream of colour seemed to be flowing down the valley towards them. When it came closer everyone could see that it was like a rainbow—a mixture of every colour under the sun. Nearer still, and they saw a million dragonflies and butterflies turning and twisting, fluttering in the sunshine, hovering on gauzy wings. Others, small and slender, clad in quieter colours, were darting round the larger insects. Flies, sandflies, gnats, scintillating beetles, butterflies and dragonflies, they all alighted on the grass.

'Who are you?' Eagle-hawk asked wonderingly.

'We are the insects that left in autumn,' they said. 'The same spirits are here to meet you, in new bodies. Crow must be right. We have gone through death and come back into a new life.'

'Yes,' said Crow softly, with none of his usual grandiloquence, 'you have indeed solved the mystery of death by showing us how the spirit can pass from one body to another, from one state of existence to one that is even more glorious.'

They came from many parts of the northern part of the continent, those Bee Men of long ago—so far back in the Dreamtime that they had little knowledge of food or how to obtain it. Those who came from the coastal lands and from the south-east were armed with spears made of sharp-pointed bamboo, and spear-throwers; a man from Melville Island had a throwing stick, a barbed spear, and a fighting stick; those who had come from the east bore stone-tipped spears and stone boomerangs. They had come together at this place to barter pearl shell and spears, hair belts and coloured ochre, grinding stones and axe-heads, boomerangs and pitcheri leaves.

A brisk trade developed until two of the men quarrelled over the exchange of gifts. Soon they were all at each other's throats. Some of the barter articles were trodden underfoot, and the weapons, spears and fighting sticks and boomerangs, they had brought to trade with were briskly employed in defence and attack. There were broken heads and limbs, and wounds from which blood poured on the sand.

There was no thought of hunting on that dreadful day. When night came, bodies lay still in death and, because they were Bee Men, the sweat still dripped from the pores of their skin. It was sweet, like honey. Ants crawled over them and picked it from them.

Only a few of the warriors remained alive and even they had changed in form. Tiny wings and hairs had sprouted from their bodies. Looking down at the dead men, they saw bees swarming in the gaping flesh.

They looked at each other in wonder. They spoke to each other in the droning voices of bees. They were joined by the spirits of the dead men. Their bodies turned to stone. Dead men and living men, they lay on the ground in the form of rounded boulders, above which swarms of bees buzzed and hovered incessantly. Their barter goods turned to stone but the spirits of the Bee Men were now all bees, tasting the pollen, storing it, making honey for the men and women who came into the world in following ages—men and women who eat honey, and flesh of animals, and birds and lizards, eggs and fish, and fruit and berries, grubs and insects and seeds and vegetables of many kinds—but of all these the honey of the bees adds something that no other food can supply.

Amongst the several principal types of folk tale is the 'play' story. It usually provides intimate details of the sexual adventures and misadventures of a cunning fellow who employs his wiles to seduce unwary women. Not infrequently the tables are turned and he becomes the victim. These tales give great enjoyment to the listeners, who are titillated as much by their scandalous element (for which there may be assumed disapproval) as by their broad humour.

One such tale from Arnhem Land includes the adventures of two sisters who went some distance from the bay where their people were camped to collect cycad palm nuts. When their dilly-bags were full they dried the nuts in the sun, pounded them, and soaked them in fresh water. They were occupied for several days in this work. When it was finished they left the pounded nuts and made a new camp some way off by a mangrove swamp where they proposed to gather periwinkles.

Seeing no sign of other people near the lonely swamp they divested themselves of their pandanus leaf skirts and waded through the mud where the mangroves were thickly clustered.

It happened that a lonely hunter was close by and saw the

women picking their way through the swamp. It was many days since he had seen a woman. Looking back, the sisters saw him standing at the edge of the swamp and hastened towards the concealment of the mangroves.

The hunter laughed, and said to himself, 'Two to choose from! Or shall I have them both?'

He took small magic articles from the wide bark belt he was wearing and used them to conjure up torrential rain that churned up the mud, making it dangerous for anyone to linger there. The hunter concealed himself behind a tree. As the women freed themselves from the clinging mud and started to race along the beach, the hunter stepped out and caught both of them by the arms.

The elder sister pulled herself free and escaped to the camp that had been set up earlier in the day. The younger woman was less fortunate. Namaranganin, the hunter, gathered the girl up in his arms. Taking no notice of her screams and struggles, he carried her bodily to his own temporary camp in the jungle.

Before they reached the tiny clearing where his camp was located, Baiangun, the other sister, had collected the cycad nut paste and had made her way back to her people's camp.

'Where is your sister?' she was asked.

'Jalmarida has been caught and carried away. I don't know where she is. Deep in the jungle somewhere, I expect.'

'Who has taken her?'

'I saw him only for a moment, when he caught hold of my arm. I pulled away from him so he was just a blur, but I think it was Namaranganin the hunter.'

The men wasted no time in gathering their weapons and setting out on the trail, following the girl's footsteps until they came to the beach near the mangrove swamp. There they saw the footprints of a heavily laden man leading into the jungle, and knew that it was Namaranganin, heavily burdened with the girl. By then it was dark. The men lit a fire and made camp for the night.

Far away in the clearing Namaranganin was making good use of Jalmarida. She gathered firewood and helped her abductor to build a shelter. When it was finished he left her there while he tried to find some bird or animal for their evening meal. There was no need to warn her to remain in the clearing.

He had taken a tortuous path after leaving the beach, and she had no idea where her people's camp might be.

Namaranganin returned with two ducks. They provided a meal for man and woman. The flames died down. The girl was dragged into the hut, but refused to comply with Namaranganin's demands.

The cunning man did not force her. He fed the fire at the opening of the hut with dry twigs, coaxing it to a blaze, then piled quantities of damp leaves on it, and lay down beside her in the stringybark hut.

During the night she asked, 'Why is the hut full of smoke?'

'To keep you awake,' he replied.

'Why?'

He laughed, 'You are a woman. You should know.'

'You've made a big mistake,' she said. 'You should have taken my sister instead of me. I'm protected by the Dagurura of my ancestor.'

Her subterfuge availed her little, for the sacred rannga* returned that night to the waterhole of its totemic ancestor.

Namaranganin's triumph was short-lived. Early in the morning the clearing was ringed with fire. Jalmarida's people had lit fires that prevented the hunter from escaping. They closed in on him and speared him to death.

As for Jalmarida, she was turned into a fly and flew away over the tree tops.†

Note:
Legends that explain the origin of animals and their various characteristics are not given here as many are contained in the companion volume, *Aboriginal Legends*.

---

* A stone which is also a totemic emblem.
† The story may sound puerile to a western reader, but is included for several reasons. The explicit details of the original narrative afforded great enjoyment to the listeners. The story of metamorphosis into an insect is unusual but, apart from this, is typical of camp-fire tales that were appreciated by listeners of all ages.

The Bird Tribe

MURKUPANG was a hairy giant who possessed great powers of magic. When he left his cave home to go hunting he commanded the river to rise up and block the entrance to prevent strangers from robbing it of the enchanted objects he kept there.

One long, hot, dry summer season his magic appeared to have deserted him. No matter how far afield he went he could find no game. Food for himself and his wife's mother, who lived nearby, was in short supply. Murkupang's appetite was gargantuan, in keeping with his size, and there was nothing left over for his mother-in-law. She was a shrewish old lady and would no doubt have told him what she thought of him if conversation had been permitted. Thinking that all he needed was a reminder, she sent two of her grandchildren (but of another son and daughter) to tell him that he had not sent her anything to eat for several days.

Unfortunately she had chosen an inopportune moment. Murkupang was starving. When the children came to the cave he seized them and ate them both. His hunger satisfied, he realised that his impulsive act was likely to bring trouble on himself. He was capable of dealing with half a dozen men at once, but if the old woman roused the clan against him, as well she might, it seemed likely that he would be overpowered and killed.

Gathering his magic implements together, he abandoned the cave where he had been living and travelled southwards until he came to a mountain that contained a cave much like the one he had left. The only drawback was that it was near the summit, far away from the river where he would have to draw water, and difficult to reach from any direction. There was an obvious way of overcoming the difficulty. Using the magic at his command, he carried the peak and the cave it contained down to the river bank and rested in it that night.

Next morning he turned northwards, still in search of game, with the mountain top obediently trailing behind him. Nearer the coast game was plentiful. Murkupang was satisfied that it would be a good neighbourhood in which to settle. He planted the peak on top of a low, flat mountain and took up residence in the cave, imagining himself safe from the vengeance of his relatives by marriage.

His mother-in-law, however, was not a woman to give up easily. Recruiting two helpers, who also possessed magic powers, she tracked him down.

'See that cave?' she said to the men who accompanied her. 'That's where he lives now. Stay here until he goes hunting. Then I'll tell you what to do next.'

Before long they saw the giant leave the cave and head in the direction of the river. When he was out of sight the old woman lit a fire, and made her helpers stand in the smoke to rid them of any smell that Murkupang might detect. Next she wrapped them round with stringybark and, chanting and waving her hands, moulded the bark to their bodies. She stepped back to admire her handiwork.

'Yes, that's fine. You look just like stringybark trees!' she said in a satisfied voice.

Coming back later in the day, laden with meat after a successful trip, Murkupang saw the fire, which was still burning, and came to investigate. He recognised his mother-in-law at a little distance and felt sure she had brought reinforcements. It would have taken keener eyes than his to see that there were two more stringybark trees on the plain.

When he came close to the cave entrance, he placed the body of one of the kangaroos he was carrying on the ground and called to his wife's mother. 'This is for you. Come and get it.' Not waiting to see whether she responded or not, he entered the cave and released his dogs, for he was still uncertain whether any of the tribespeople were there or not.

The dogs raced down the hillside. They searched everywhere, even passing the two stringybark trees, but could not discover any man-scent.

Satisfied at last, Murkupang led them back to the cave where he cooked a meal for himself, threw the bones to his dogs, and went to sleep.

As soon as it was dark the disguised men shed their bark coverings and carried them to the cave where they used them to block the entrance.

Taking firesticks that the old woman had concealed, they set fire to the bark. Fanned by the wind the flames roared into the cave.

Murkupang sat up, to find himself engulfed in fire and smoke. He tried to force himself through the burning bark, but was forced back by the heat. There was only one thing left to do. Using the last of his magic power, he changed himself into a mopoke and flew out through a gap in the flaming bark.

It was the end of Murkupang the hairy giant and the beginning of Murkupang the mopoke that flies stealthily in the night to avoid its enemies, crying mournfully because of the loss of the power it once had.

In Aldo Massola's account of this Mara legend he quotes a version by R. H. Matthews which says that eight dogs also escaped in the form of the soldier bird, mynah, magpie, black jay, crow, cockatoo, eagle-hawk and quail-hawk.

Emu and Jabiru

EMU and his son-in-law Jabiru the Stork were expert spear-makers. Emu specialised in the hooked variety while Jabiru made the many-pronged spear used by fishermen. The Emus and Jabirus lived together very happily, sharing the spoils of the hunt. As might be expected, Jabiru concentrated on spearing fish while Emu hunted birds and animals on land.

Early one morning Jabiru and his wife went out in their canoe to fish for stingray. They promised to bring some back for Emu and his wife. It was a successful morning's fishing. The canoe returned well laden with stringray of all sizes. While Jabiru prepared the fish for cooking, his wife lined the earth oven with stones, which were soon red-hot. When they were ready Jabiru placed the liver and fat of the fish on a piece of bark and gave them to his wife to cook.

After they had feasted on these delicacies to their hearts' content, the woman said, 'I'll take some now to my parents,' but was surprised to find nothing but flesh.

'Where's the liver and the fat?' she asked.

'All gone,' her husband said with a broad smirk. 'You didn't think there'd be any left after the big feed we've just had, did you?'

'Never mind,' she replied. 'We've often given my parents all the tasty pieces. There's plenty of flesh left. It won't do them any harm to go without the liver and fat for once.'

Unfortunately her father didn't agree.

'Where's the liver? and the fat?' he asked so fiercely that his daughter shrank back and said, 'There wasn't any. These fish didn't have any.'

'You're lying! You and that precious husband of yours have been stuffing your bellies with them. I can see the fat running down your chin. Don't I always save some of the best part of the meat for you when I go hunting?'

He snatched up his club and a handful of spears and rushed over to Jabiru, yelling, 'I'll show you what happens to those who insult me. Stand still and I'll pound the liver out of you!'

Jabiru didn't wait to have his liver pounded. He picked up a stout branch of pandanus, struck Emu's club aside, and smashed the branch into Emu's body, first on the left side and then on the right.

Emu staggered to his feet and hurled one of his spears at his daughter's husband. It penetrated his body and stuck out of his mouth. Frantic with pain, Jabiru flew away with the spear sticking out of his mouth.

They never saw each other again. Emu went inland, his wings short and stubby after being broken by the pandanus log, while Jabiru made a new home for himself in the swamp where he found his new beak useful for spearing fish.

The Tail of Willy Wagtail

IT may be hard to believe, but long ago Willy Wagtail was big and strong with a tail like that of all the other birds. He was something of a bully, too, and suspected of all kinds of crimes. In fact rumours of his addiction to cannibalism were circulated so freely that the Bram-bram-bult brothers sent one of their relatives, Tortoise, to check up on him. It was a good choice, for he was well protected with shields, back and front, if Wagtail ventured to attack him.

Tortoise approached the Wagtail camp cautiously and greeted the bird, asking if he could stay with him for a while.

Once established there, Tortoise commenced his investigations, poking into concealed corners of the gunyah and fossicking through piles of rubbish. At first his search proved unfruitful, but on the second day he came upon a number of bones underneath a pile of leaves and branches.

'What are these?' he asked.

'You can see for yourself,' Willy Wagtail said rudely. 'What did you think they were?'

Before Tortoise had time to reply, Willy Wagtail seized him by the neck, pushed him along a faint track in the bush and with a tremendous heave sent him rolling over and over. There was a sound of splintering wood and Tortoise found himself hurtling into a deep pit, straight towards a pointed stake. He twisted his body sideways to avoid it. The front of his shield was broken as it touched the stake, but otherwise he was unharmed, though somewhat bruised and shaken by the fall.

Feeling sure that Tortoise was dead, or at least mortally injured, Willy Wagtail went back to his camp to fetch his knife, intending to cut Tortoise into pieces and feast himself on them. While he was away, Tortoise managed to scramble out of the pit. He limped back to the Bram-bram-bult brothers, and told them what had befallen him.

'That proves it,' one of the brothers said. 'No wonder so many birds and animals have disappeared lately. It seems he throws them in the pit where they're impaled on the stake so he can deal with them at his leisure. Come, brother, tomorrow we're going to pay a visit to Willy Wagtail and teach him a lesson he won't easily forget.'

The Bram-bram-bults were strongly built and agile, and had no fear of the bullying Willy Wagtail. When they arrived, he eyed them doubtfully, but decided he could deal with each separately. He welcomed them and invited them to stay the night, promising to prepare a place for them to sleep.

After they had eaten, the big bird invited one of the brothers to come with him for a stroll through the bush. He went willingly, but took particular care to keep his eyes on the track, ready to detect the brushwood that concealed the death pit. Willy Wagtail led the way. When they were close to the pit, he said, 'It's your turn to go first. You go on, and I'll follow.'

Instead of replying the Bram-bram-bult gave him a push that sent him reeling back, on to the pile of brushwood. Willy Wagtail stumbled, tried to save himself, and with a despairing cry, disappeared into the hole. The second brother came running along the path. Together they looked down. There was Willy Wagtail, lying helplessly at the bottom, his back broken by the wicked stake.

They pulled him out, carried him back to the camp, and chanted spells to make him shrink into a bird so small that he would not be able to harm anyone. In time Willy Wagtail recovered from his broken back, but his tail refused to straighten itself.

And, if you look, you will see that Tortoise still has a chip out of his carapace.

The habits and characteristics of curlews and owls, which are the subject of a number of legends, are summed up in a Narunga legend from the York Peninsula.

Long ago Owl was a man who lived in a cave by the seashore. He had no wife, but was very fond of his two dogs. Close by, on the beach, lived Curlew with his wife and children, who were left at home when their parents were hunting.

One day Mopoke was walking along the beach and saw the children playing on the sand.

'Look, there's a meal for you,' he said to his dogs.

Later that day the Curlews returned to their camp. There were no children waiting to greet them—only an untidy heap of gnawed bones. They knew at once what had happened. Their wailing cry, the cry that curlews still make, reached the ears of Mopoke who was sitting in his cave, with the well-fed dogs crouched at his feet.

Mopoke prepared for an attack by Curlew, but as the days went by without any sign of his enemy, he relaxed his precautions.

Curlew was biding his time. Revenge would be all the sweeter if delayed. He wanted to make sure it would be effective, for Mopoke was stronger than he.

The opportunity arrived when he happened to meet Kangaroo.

'You can help me,' he said, and told his friend of the terrible thing Mopoke had done.

Appalled by the account of this ruthless deed, Kangaroo responded as Curlew had hoped. 'You can count on me,' he said.

'This is what I want you to do,' said Curlew, and told him of the plan he had concocted. 'I want you to browse on the plants near Mopoke's cave. Pretend you haven't seen it. I'm sure that he'll want to kill you when he knows you're there, especially if he thinks you can be taken unawares. He'll be sure to set one of his dogs on you. When it gets near, run into the scrub and hide.'

'I can do that,' Kangaroo said, 'but how will that help you? What will you be doing?'

'I'll be hiding too. When the dog rushes at you, he'll get the surprise of his life.'

'That won't really settle the score with Mopoke, will it?' Kangaroo asked.

Curlew smiled through the tears that still ran down his face. He assured his friend that it was only the beginning.

Kangaroo cooperated, and the plan worked out just as Curlew had promised. He was so well hidden, close to where Kangaroo was browsing, that the dog had no idea he was there. As it rushed past, Curlew clubbed it on the head, and dragged it down to the beach.

Mopoke was mystified. He had seen the dog running down the hill and disappearing in the scrub, while Kangaroo, who appeared to have taken fright, hid himself, but presently reappeared and went on eating as though nothing had happened.

He released his second dog, and again it failed to return.

That night Mopoke felt sad. Both his dogs had disappeared without trace, and he had no wife to comfort him. He spent a lonely and unpleasant night.

In the morning he heard someone calling him. It was Curlew, who was standing on the cliff top above his cave, taunting him, calling on him to come out and fight.

It is difficult to realise the despair of an old bachelor who has lost his only friends, even though they are only dogs. He had no stomach for fighting. All he wanted was to be left alone, to brood over the loss of his four-footed companions.

When the challenge remained unanswered, Curlew cursed the killer of his children.

> 'Remain in your cave for ever,' he shouted.
> 'Sulk there today and every day.
> You'll never see the sun again.
> You'll be afraid to come out in the
>   daytime lest I am lying in wait
>   to kill you.
> You'll have to wait till dark to hunt
>   for food.
> You'll have no friends because you're
>   a creature of the dark.
> The only living creatures you'll see
>   will be the little ones you
>   kill in the dark.
> Remain in your cave for ever!'

That is why mopokes live in caves and hidden places, venturing forth only at night.

It was a fitting punishment for one who fed helpless children to his dogs, but it did not lessen the grief of Curlew and his wife, who will always mourn for their dead children.

The Discovery of Fire

EVERY tribe had its own version of the origin of fire. The versions have a certain uniformity. An animal of some species gains possession of the fire and refuses to part with it. After various skirmishes it is taken from its guardian, by guile or by force, and distributed to those who have need of it. The first example comes from Victoria, the second from the Northern Territory.

Two women belonging to a tribe that lived near the present city of Melbourne were endeavouring to extract honey from an ants' nest when they were attacked by a swarm of snakes. They fought desperately, striking at them with their fighting sticks. One of them missed the snake at which it was aimed and struck a boulder, breaking in two. A sheet of flame flew out of one of the broken ends. A Crow that was perched on an overhanging branch was fascinated by the unusual sight. It swooped down, snatched the broken piece up in its beak, and sped away. While the women were still trying to kill the snakes, two men happened to see the trail of smoke left by the Crow as it flew overhead. They ran after it as fast as they could, shouting and throwing stones at it. The startled Crow dropped the stick, which fell into the long grass and started a conflagration.

The Great Father, Punjel, took the men to his home in the sky and told them that the gift of fire must never be allowed to go out. He showed them how to use it to cook food and warm themselves on cold nights, warning them that it must never be allowed to break loose again. They paid heed to his words, but after a while grew careless and allowed their campfire to die. Soon the world was as fireless as before the fire came from the woman's fighting stick.

No sooner was the gift lost than all the tribespeople realised how dependent they had become on the gift of Punjel. In addition, the snakes, who had been repelled by fire, multiplied and attacked the people in their camps and gunyahs.

Seeing what was happening, Pallyang, another celestial deity, sent his sister, Karakarook, to earth to defend women who were molested by snakes when they left their camps to dig for yams.

Karakarook's enormous fighting stick made short work of the snakes until it broke. Once again the flame came from the broken stick, and again Crow pounced on it and flew away with it.

Punjel lifted the men who had previously chased the Crow, and placed them on a mountain top. The Crow flew into their outstretched arms, and the firestick was wrested from it.

Karakarook gave her broken stick to the women, while the men who had captured the fire instructed their fellow tribesmen how to make and use firesticks.

'Punjel warns you that this is the last chance you will have to preserve fire,' they told the men who had gathered on the mountain top. 'But because he wishes you well, we will teach you how to make fire by rubbing two sticks together in a special way.'

Little Hawk, Big Hawk, and Dog lived together near the Daly River. Dog's principal duty was to supply yams, for he had the gift of scenting the buried roots and digging them up with his strong paws.

One day he came back with a good supply and said, 'Let's light a fire and cook them for our evening meal.'

'We haven't got any fire,' Little Hawk said.

'I know that as well as you do,' Dog retorted. 'It's easy to get fire. All you have to do is to take a pointed stick, press it against another piece of wood, and twirl it round till the fire comes.'

'You're the strongest,' Big Hawk said. 'If it's so easy, you do it. Then we'll know how to do it another time. Here's a pointed stick.'

Dog took the stick and twirled it vigorously between his paws, but no smoke or fire came from it. When his paws became sore, he gave up, saying 'It's no good. I haven't learned to do it properly. We'll have to get a firestick.'

'Where do we get a firestick from?'

'There are some women over there,' he said, indicating a camp some distance away. 'All you have to do is to bring back a firestick from their campfire.'

'They're bigger than we are,' Little Hawk objected. 'If you go they'll be too frightened to refuse.'

'Very well,' said the obliging Dog, and limped away on his sore paws. When he reached the camp, he watched the women preparing the ovens, and asked for a firestick. They refused to give him one and went on with their work. Dog decided to take one by force. He waited until the fire blazed up in the oven and bounded over to it. The women pushed him away, refusing to let him near the fire.

Dog returned dejectedly to his friends and confessed he had been unable to get a firestick.

'We'll have to sneak up quietly, and get it when they're not looking,' he told his friends. 'I'm too big. What about you, Little Hawk? You're small. They'd never notice you.'

'All right,' Little Hawk said, and went to the women's camp, where he hid behind a pandanus to see what they were doing.

The meal was over, and the fire was out. He waited there, all night, while the women slept; all day, while they went out to gather fresh supplies of food. Drowsing in the dusk he was wakened by movement close to his hiding place. The women were searching for Dog and his friend Big Hawk whom they suspected might have come to steal their fire, but Little Hawk was so small they failed to notice him standing in the shadow of the pandanus. As soon as the fire burned up he darted over to it, and snatched a blazing stick.

As he flew back to Big Hawk and Dog, pieces of charcoal fell from the stick, leaving traces along the track that can still be seen. When he arrived at the camp, he found that Dog had become tired of waiting and had eaten the yams he had collected without having them cooked.

Little Hawk was annoyed to think that he had spent so much time and, at the end, risked his life to provide Dog with the fire he wanted, only to find he had eaten his food raw.

He scolded his friend unmercifully. Dog was too ashamed to reply—which accounts for the fact that dogs no longer chatter as chicken-hawks do, and eat their food raw.